*Ottakar's* LOCAL HISTORY *Series*

# Aberystwyth

*Militia Barracks, c. 1910.*

*Ottakar's* LOCAL HISTORY *Series*

# Aberystwyth

*Compiled by*
Inge Manning

TEMPUS

First published 2001
Copyright © Ottakar's, 2001

Ottakar's Local History Series
produced in association with
Tempus Publishing Limited
The Mill, Brimscombe Port,
Stroud, Gloucestershire, GL5 2QG

ISBN 0 7524 2298 7

Typesetting and origination by
Tempus Publishing Limited
Printed in Great Britain by
Midway Colour Print, Wiltshire

*Angel Inn, upper Great Darkgate Street, 1910.*

# Contents

# Introduction

Like it or loathe it, we all live in a world of international markets, instantaneous communications and increasingly remote government, characterized by the ugly term 'globalization'. Nevertheless, in Wales most people still live fairly close to where they were born or moved to as children. There is still a strong attachment to place and family. Many incomers have also sought to identify closely with their new towns or villages.

The topography, society and economy of most modern communities are a product of their history. A knowledge and appreciation of local history strengthens a person's sense of community and attachment to the place. Moreover, an intelligent, comparative study of such history also helps the individual to understand the place of their local society in the broader history of their region or nation. It can reinforce their love of home while counteracting any tendency to narrow parochialism based on misleading myths and distorted memory.

Professional historians now fully appreciate the importance of local history in illuminating issues of regional, national or even international history, and many of them are engaged in precisely this kind of research. However, the subject is so vast that there is plenty of scope for the amateur to make significant contributions. To enter this field does require the adoption of professional standards in the use of evidence, but there are many books to help one get started and a plethora of courses are available.

Not everyone aspires to writing a professional-style history, and there is no need to do so to gain enjoyment and knowledge. The act of studying old records or talking to witnesses can bring the pleasure of discovering the unexpected facts about one's family, house and surroundings. Writing these discoveries down then brings this knowledge to a wider audience.

Ottakar's has shown considerable enterprise in sponsoring a 'Write your own local history' competition and publishing the entries with Tempus Publishing. As can be seen from the contents of this book, the competition has encouraged entrants to address a wide range of themes in the history of Aberystwyth and Ceredigion.

Personal reminiscences form an important section of the book; these are both history in themselves and potential sources for other local historians. Topics include holidaying in rural Cardiganshire before the Second World War, changes in farming, Aberystwyth as a holiday resort and related memories of the 1930s and '40s, memories of the first aeroplane to land in Goginan, and musings on the social changes visible in Aberystwyth from the 1970s to the present. Family history, house history and the use of local sources all illustrate a fundamental theme running through the town's past: the sea.

The topographical setting of Aberystwyth and its hinterland and the vicissitudes of nature are described in two short pieces. Several authors describe from various standpoints the history of the town and its neighbouring villages: Pen Dinas Iron Age hill-fort, Llanbadarn, Aberystwyth Castle, changing views of the town, its economic basis, and Penparcau. More specific contributions deal with transport, an unsavoury incident in the history of the Royal Mail in the town, and the life of an important painter of Aberystwyth scenes, Alfred Worthington.

Aspects of Cardiganshire history outside Abeystwyth are considered in a history of Cwmystwyth school, a description of the hat makers of Tre'r Ddol, a general history of dairy farming in the county, and the diary of an English lady's visit in 1822.

Ottakar's and the contributors are to be congratulated for bringing this fascinating glimpse of Aberystwyth's history to fruition. I hope that it will encourage others to take up the study of local history for the benefit of their community and for their own pleasure.

David M. Browne MA, FRAI, FRGS
July 2001

# Acknowledgements

I would like to thank Ottakar's and all the contributors to this book. I have enjoyed this project enormously, not only was it extremely interesting to discover the wealth of material which was made available, but I have met many interesting people in the course of its production, all of whom went out of their way help me as a complete novice.

I would particularly like to thank the following: Williams Howells from Ceredigion Public Library; and William Troughton from the National Library, who were extremely helpful and knowledgeable. William Troughton is the author of *Aberystwyth Voices* and was therefore a valuable ally. He has also kindly donated two pieces for the book.

Ron Cowell, Chairman of the Postcard Collector's Club in Aberystwyth, who allowed me to choose from a wide selection of postcards he made available from his collection. He has also contributed a piece.

David Browne, from the Royal Commission on the Ancient Historical Monuments of Wales, a very experienced editor and writer, who not only contributed to the book, but also wrote the introduction and judged the competition.

Inge Manning
July 2001

# CHAPTER 1

# A tour of the Area

*Great Darkgate Street and North Parade, showing the clock tower in 1905.*

## Aberystwyth Town Walls

Although Aberystwyth has not had town walls for at least 300 years, a walk around the boundaries of the old settlement reminds us of many aspects of the town's history. The walk, if taken as a gentle stroll, should take in the region of an hour. It is unlikely that even Edward I envisaged that parts of his castle would still be standing over 700 years later; nor that the vision his planners had, when the town's charter was granted in 1277, would still govern the plan of the town. The walls isolated the slightly elevated land on which the oldest parts of Aberystwyth were built. They also served to isolate the settlers that Edward I moved into the area around the castle from the potentially

hostile native hordes.

One of the more obvious manifestations of the medieval street plan is the name 'Great Darkgate Street'. It is so named because it was at the junction of Great Darkgate Street with Chalybeate Street and Baker Street that the main gateway through the town walls stood, flanked by two round towers. This is commemorated by a plaque on the wall of the Halifax bank, which itself stands on the site of the old house of correction, built in the era when transgressors of the law would be tied to a cart and whipped as they were paraded through the streets.

To follow the line of the old town walls, turn into Chalybeate Street which, like most of the town built on the flat land to the north of the Great Dark Gate, is of nineteenth century origin. Aberystwyth became a popular resort with the gentry during the Napoleonic wars. Being unable to go on their grand tours of continental Europe, those of means were forced to look closer to home for their entertainment and Aberystwyth proved ideal. Many of the other resorts popular with the better-off were able to offer spa waters, with restorative powers able to cure a variety of illnesses. Fortunately for Aberystwyth such a spring just happened to be found near the present-day railway station. An early nineteenth-century analysis of the water from the well described it as being 'neither acidulous nor saline (except after high tides when it has been mixed with sea water), but simply chalybeate and is by no means unpalatable'. Potential supplicants were no doubt further reassured by the assertions that 'nitrate of barytes does not indicate the presence of sulphuric acid' and 'syrup of violets, after standing for some time, becomes very slightly green.' They may however have been alarmed to read that 'to persons of a delicate habit the fresh drawn water may, from its low temperature, occasion an unpleasant sensation in the stomach,' or, even worse, 'chalybeate waters when first employed frequently evacuate the bowels...' Not an overriding endorsement! In order to ensure that such a useful resource did not escape the notice of visitors, the name Chalybeate Street was adopted even though the connection between the street and the spring is at best tenuous.

A stroll down Chalybeate Street a hundred years ago would have taken you past the Llyn Vango refreshment rooms, Teece the grocer, the Sewing Machine Depot (proprietor John Brutus Davies), Evan Lewis cab proprietor and Northey's Commercial Hotel. In more recent times John Williams the fishmonger was a popular institution in the town. Chalybeate Street is bisected by another street, which at one time would have ended abruptly at the town walls. Over the years this street has been known as Barkers Lane, Lurkers Lane, Heol Y Moch (reflecting the fact that the pig market was once conducted at the top of the street) and now Queen Street.

At the end of Chalybeate Street, pause for a moment and look down Alexandra Road. The area in front of you used to be a wet and marshy tract. In front of the railway station (the present façade built in 1925 has been refurbished and is Aberystwyth's newest pub), stood Waterloo Bridge, which spanned the Mill Leet, which comprised the Penglais and Plascrug streams. The roundabout in front of us marks the site of another bridge, Corry Bridge, that spanned the same stream. During the Civil War Aberystwyth housed a mint producing silver coinage for the Royalist cause. This aroused the interest of the Roundheads who, in January 1644, entered Llanbadarn with fifty men. With the intention of surprising the men, a smaller number of Royalists set off on a dawn raid, but were routed by the Roundheads. In the confusion that followed thirteen of the Royalists were drowned in this area as they fled.

Turn right past the Shell garage into Mill Street. The Welsh name for Mill Street, Dan Dre literally means 'underneath the town', alluding to the fact that here we are just outside the walls of the old town. Across the street a large wooden door is sometimes left ajar. Through the door can be seen sparks arcing and curving, clawing their way through the gloom. This is the Cambrian Forge and has been in the hands of the Lewis family for over eighty years. Beyond the Shell garage is a terrace of three buildings. All three have been public houses at one time or another. The first is still called the Plough and was a public house until twenty or so years ago. Next to it was the Red Lion, though it is well over a century since the last pint was pulled there. The last of the trio is the Mill Inn, formerly the Cross Foxes. Across George Street we see the imposing Tabernacle Chapel, built in 1878 with seating for 1,500 people.

At the far end of Mill Street is the old Town Mill. Apart from the castle, this building may well be the oldest building in Aberystwyth, though it has been expanded and rebuilt numerous times as the town has grown. Inhabitants of the town were compelled to have their corn ground at the mill. A proportion of this corn was retained and used to finance the running of St Mary's Chapel. St Mary's has long ago vanished under the waves. Bridge Street was for centuries the commercial hub of Aberystwyth. This was because much of the traffic came into Aberystwyth through Trefechan, across the Rheidol and through a gate in the town wall and into Bridge Street. The town walls ran from here approximately along the length of South Road, known by the far more descriptive name of Shipbuilders Row during the nineteenth century. However it is more interesting to take a diversion here and cross Mill Street, head towards the river and turn right under Trefechan Bridge.

The current Trefechan Bridge is at its most spectacular when viewed from underneath. It was built during the 1880s after a flood in 1886 washed away its predecessor. The architect was Sir J.W. Szlumper who lived in Sandmarsh Cottage in Queens Road and was also responsible for the Vale of Rheidol Railway. The builder was David Lloyd. Despite being designed for little more than horses and carts, the bridge copes well with juggernauts, beyond the realms of fantasy of those who built the bridge.

On the right hand side is Rummers Wine Bar, another old building that has served as a grain store, theatre, chandler's and china shop. Walking past the sewage works, we come to that area of the harbour known as the Gap. In days gone by this area was known as Y Geulan and was the centre of the shipbuilding industry in Aberystwyth. It was always regarded as a community within a community as it was here that those who made their living from the sea lived. The area once boasted timber yards, sail lofts, chain and anchor smiths, block makers and many more related crafts that, between 1824 and 1882, built 189 sailing vessels. The names given, christened with a bottle of port smashed on the bow and launched on waves of optimism, evoke a bygone era and are recorded in the Shipping Registers kept in the County Record Office: Ocean Child, Cambrian Belle, Alert, Claudia, Progress, Confidence, John Elias, Messenger and Desdemona to name a few. The name Aberystwyth was familiar all over the globe. To many local sailors the streets of ports on the other side of the world were more familiar than the villages outside Aberystwyth. Just to remind us of our own mortality, the same Shipping Registers succinctly detail the fate of the vessels: Lost all hands, Milford; Sold Portugal; Condemned Jamaica; Wrecked Buenos Aires; Disappeared; Missing....

Take the broad set of steps next to Tanycae Sunday School, up onto South Road, once called Shipwrights Row. The house on your left was once the Sailors Arms; the Chain and Anchor and Shipwrights Arms were close by.

The walk deviates from the town walls here as we walk up Prospect Street, where many of the cottages reflect their former occupiers' links to the sea; names such as Moel-y-Don and Batavia are some surviving examples. Examination of the surrounding streets will provide plenty more. From the top of Prospect Street, turn left into St Michael's Place. It is difficult to imagine the castle as it was in its heyday, with concentric rings of unassailable walls gleaming white and malevolent at the subdued natives. Edward I liked his castles

*Aberystwyth College, 1895.*

*Victoria Terrace and Constitution Hill c. 1910.*

*Bridge Street, late 1960s.*

painted in lime wash so they stood out. So unassailable were the walls that the castle only fell into enemy hands as a result of treachery. Today little remains of the castle when compared with others from the same era such as Harlech and Caernarfon. This is due to two reasons: firstly the use of gunpowder after the Civil War to destroy the castle and, more importantly, the use of the discarded masonry by the inhabitants for building houses in the town. The idea of recycling is not new in Aberystwyth.

Incidentally the town walls went the same way. An anonymous commentator, writing in 1816, described the castle as 'a clay cold mouldering monument of ancient grandeur'. The castle is worthy of a walk in its own right. Vandals permitting, there are numerous plaques and information boards to help explore and understand the layout of the castle.

From St Michael's Place turn left into Upper Great Darkgate Street. Here is another building exuding grandeur, the Assembly Rooms, built for the gentry to entertain themselves. Designed by Thomas Repton and opened in 1820, they were used for balls, promenades, card playing, musical concerts

and billiards. They were an instant success. In the early years of the twentieth century the building served as the first National Library of Wales. Further down we come to the old meat market in St James Square. Such was the popularity of the market that during the last century St James Square boasted no less than twelve pubs – Albion, Angel, Australia Vaults, Black Swan, Farmers Arms, Lord Nelson, Royal Oak, Ship Aground, Ship and Castle, Ship in Launch, Three Jolly Sailors, and the White Swan.

Continue walking down Upper Great Darkgate Street and you come to the town clock. This is not the original town clock but a replacement, built in 2000 after a gap of forty-four years. Much to the displeasure of the townsfolk, the local council took a reprehensible decision that only council committees can make and chose to demolish the ninety-nine-year-old clock in 1956. The habit of townsfolk of still issuing directions involving the town clock has caused much confusion over the decades.

From the town clock, turn left into Pier Street. Before walking too far, look at the windows above the Penguin Café. Two distinct styles are to be seen. The oldest are the Georgian curved windows, once seen throughout the town. In another of their inexplicable decisions, the council decided that these were not modern enough. Stipulations were placed on all leasehold properties to the effect that when a lease came to an end new sash windows would have to be installed in place of their Georgian counterparts. Continue along Pier Street until the junction with Eastgate. On the corner shop look for the plaque commemorating the fact that the writer Alfred Noyes lived here during his youth. Proceed down Eastgate a short way and you will see a public house, Downie's Vaults, named after Joseph Downie, a bank manager, wine and spirit merchant and philanthropist, who lived on the site of the pub. Immediately to the right of the pub is a narrow alleyway. Walk down the alleyway until you reach Windmill Court, a terrace of abandoned cottages. These are typical of the houses lived in by the ordinary folk of Aberystwyth a century and more ago. Eastgate, Great Darkgate Street and Queen Street had a number of these small courts with their substandard housing. In 1881, thirty-one people lived in the seven cottages that comprised Windmill Court. From here backtrack to the junction with Pier Street and walk towards the sea. At the bottom of Pier Street turn right onto the promenade. Before returning to the old town walls pause for a moment and view some of the impressive buildings, or have an ice cream from the Pier. Facing the Pier is the Theological College, originally built as the Hotel Cambria, which failed spectacularly in 1905, and was purchased for conversion to a Presbyterian Theological College. It was owned by the Aberystwyth Improvement Company, who also owned the Pier and Cliff Railway. The pier itself was built in the 1860s, but it was the Aberystwyth Improvement Company which renamed it the Royal Pier after a visit by Princess Alexandra to open the pavilion. They also built the Cliff Railway. While looking towards Constitution Hill, note the shelter built on a slight promontory jutting into the sea. This was the site of the gallows in times gone by.

Proceed along the promenade towards Constitution Hill. Opposite the paddling pool is a small café. Turn right behind this café and you will be confronted by a flight of steep stone steps. These marked the third of the four gates through the town walls. It was down these steps that felons were marched on the way to the aforementioned gallows. At the top of the steps follow the row of fishermen's cottages. At the junction of Crynfryn Row and Crynfryn Buildings, stood the last vestiges of the town walls. They were to be seen until the 1880s or so. From here turn left, then right into Alfred Place. Facing you is a statue of a young Queen Victoria. This was once a ship's figurehead but how it arrived on the wall of the then Victoria Hotel is a mystery. The bottom of Eastgate marked the final of the four gates through the town wall. Until a century ago the street was known as Little Darkgate Street, attesting to this fact. The name was changed to address the concerns of the street's shopkeepers who felt they were losing trade because of the name Little Darkgate. Keep walking and you will return to the bottom of Great Darkgate Street where the walk commenced.

*William Troughton*

# CHAPTER 2

## *Personal Memories*

*Mrs A. Evans' grandmother's house in Pontrhydfendigaid.*

## Nana's House

Even today when I think of Paddington station it evokes that stab of excitement that signalled the start of my childhood holidays in Wales. We went to the Isle of Wight and to France, but nothing equalled the thrill of leaving the noise and sootiness of London to travel to my grandmother's house in Wales, which happened about twice a year, every year, until my teens.

The journey, several hours of mounting excitement, took us through the Home Counties towards the Bristol Channel, through the Severn Tunnel and on towards Carmarthen. Thereafter, it always seemed to

me that we entered a different, magical, greener world. A beautiful place of incomparably sweet-smelling air, which I would inhale in huge lungfuls with my head stuck out of the train window.

Somewhere during the latter part of the journey waiters in starched white jackets would walk along the corridors, calling 'Tea now being served.' In the dining car tables were laid with cloths and a full tea of sandwiches, scones, cakes and tea was served to us. On the carriage compartment walls, posters extolled the exaggerated charms of places like Clacton, Margate, Torquay, depicting golden sands (always) and tanned lithe-bodied figures playing beach ball. Beneath these colourful posters, netted hammocks stretched and held packages and small bags. The seats were upholstered in a particularly scratchy fabric that smelled to me of horse manure and tobacco.

As the train left Tregaron to travel across the huge bog of Cors Caron with its backdrop of the Cambrian Mountains, we would begin to gather together our belongings (which included cats in cat baskets when Grandmother was travelling) in readiness for our destination, the tiny station of Strata Florida. The great clattering steam train puffed and slid into the station where Dick Jones, flat cap at a jaunty angle and big smile at the ready, waited to greet us, escort us across the track after the train had pulled out, and onward to Aberystwyth. In wintertime he held aloft a storm lantern and led us to one of his two old cars – roomy, stylish, with walnut dash and cracked leather seats.

If I ever travelled on my own, once in the car Dick would let rip in song, mostly in Welsh and with strong encouragements to join in. This sing-song culminated with perfect timing in 'She'll be coming 'round the mountain when she comes', to coincide with the moment we rounded the final bend up the mountain and my Grandmother's house came into view. The house was called 'in the hollow of the white birches'. It was always the high point of the whole journey and the memory of it still thrills. If, as was more usually the case, I was travelling with my mother or other family members, Dick's renditions were more muted, *sotto-voce* – though nonetheless melodious as he had a fine baritone voice – and always punctuated by rich chuckles.

One particular little scenario was played out every arrival, every year, without

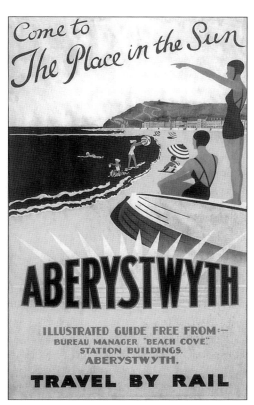

*Poster of museum's collection, 1938.*

exception and it went as follows. Dick, with a straight face but twinkling eyes, would ask whether I preferred living in London or Pontrhydfendigaid. There was of course only one possible answer, to which he produced his great roar of laughter and slapped his leg, as if it were the best joke in the world and the first time he'd heard it. What a dear man he was.

On arrival at the house, Nana would emerge to greet us (having no doubt watched out for us for a long while) and Dick, assuming the more serious demeanour of a chauffeur, carried in the luggage. After his departure, we'd settle at once in the big old kitchen where, with oil lamps burning, Tilley lamp hissing, fire

15

*Anna Evans.*

crackling in the grate and food on the table, I would sink into the chair and know that I had once again returned to the place that I loved most.

My Grandmother was a gregarious, creative woman who, once widowed, found herself having to live many of her later years in long periods of isolation in the large old Welsh house; she who enjoyed people, shops, theatres and all the facilities of city life. Consequently, when company did find its way to her, she was unstoppable. Out poured stories, news, questions, answers, opinions, anecdotes and gossip, all jostling for space. Local scandals, births, marriages and deaths fought with enquiries about London life in general and family news in particular. It would be another twenty years before the telephone came to this house, too late for Nana. We talked into the night until, all topics spent for the moment, we'd fill hot water bottles, bank up the fire, light candles, extinguish the lamps and make our way up to bed. I realized, while thinking about it recently, that in all the years there

we never locked the doors at night. Whatever for? Later, lying in the feather bed in my room above the warm kitchen (the room where I was born) I'd watch the dancing shadows cast from the candlelight and contemplate, in a state of almost perfect contentment, the long days of holiday ahead, eventually falling into a deep and peaceful sleep.

It was the raddling of the kitchen range directly beneath me that awoke me to the first day of the holidays. A clearly remembered sound is that of the pantry door opening; because it lay flush against the stone floor it dragged open with a 'whoomph' sound, which indicated that the preparations of breakfast had begun. One of my first jobs was to take a large jug through the house to the connecting farmhouse via a long, dark passage and there get it filled up with fresh, foamy milk. I loved the slightly scary feeling of hurrying through that passage, which I recall was lined on one side with shelves filled with ancient pots, pans and kitchen implements of a bygone time. In the farmhouse kitchen I stood transfixed, staring up at the sides of bacon hanging from hooks in the beams, salted and smoked bacon, which tasted sublime. Never, ever since, has bacon tasted as good as that which was carved off in thick slices and eaten with fresh bread from a large round loaf.

Another job I enjoyed was taking the two water cans to the pipe amongst the ferns at the back of the house where the spring emerged from the rock, to be filled up for the day's use. Outside a wonderful world stirred to life and beckoned me. I could hardly wait to rediscover my special haunts and all the old familiar places and things, always there, precious, unchanged, providing a wonderful stability and continuity throughout my childhood. Most of the time I played on my own, inhabiting a kingdom I had created, whose headquarters lay under vast, cavernous rhododendron bushes below the front lawns. Dolls and teddies were carted down to this base-camp in an old orange box on wheels that served well as a pram for many years. Tea parties took place there and when this palled a bit, a swing on the entrance gate diverted. Or, better still, perched up high on one of the stone pillars that flanked the gate, I would act as a lookout for any suspicious sightings and write down these mysterious observations in cryptic code. This gave excitement to warm drowsy afternoons that saw little activity beyond the buzzing of dragonflies and bees, or the scudding of puffy white clouds across an azure sky.

In those days the arrival of a car was an event of major excitement. We could hear it approaching before we could actually see it come around the curve of beeches that lined the drive to the house. The sound of the approaching vehicle always caused near panic; it signalled visitors and therefore meant dropping whatever you were doing to hastily discard aprons, comb hair, put the kettle on, or whatever. For me, it meant diving into the nearest ferns or rhododendrons to spy on the hapless visitors. Nana, being deaf, had to be informed of the arrival and, whoever they were, they would probably be treated to the best china, the silver teapot and tea in the drawing room. This was torture for me, dragged in from my precious adventures and freedom, to have to sit on the edge of a hard settee and listen to polite conversation, but such occasions were not all that frequent. Down by the river I had discovered two caves opposite each other near a rickety old wooden bridge, but in all my childhood years I never managed to summon the courage to investigate them. Years later when I took my own children to see them, we discovered that they were not really caves at all, but just shallow inlets in the rocks.

At dusk I loved to run, leap and dance up and down the drive, then at last to watch the sun setting behind the woods. Then, as the light faded and it became chilly I'd close the gate and run back to the house as fast as I could and once inside, begin lighting up the lamps for the evening.

Bus trips to town were dreaded, due to my chronic travel-sickness. The journey to Aberystwyth took about an hour because it stopped on request at every cottage and farm on the twelve-mile journey – or so it seemed. It was complete misery to have to ask the driver on occasion to stop whilst I dismounted and, watched with great interest by the entire bus, took great gulps of fresh air and clambered back, ashen-faced to continue the journey. At a certain place about four miles from town the bus had to strain laboriously up a very steep hill, before levelling out at a high point on the top. Just about here, the first distant glimpse of the memorial chimney signified that the journey was nearly over; the constant ones stopping and starting and ghastly fumes about to end. At this same spot was a farm, set back from the road, and each week on the same day the farmer's wife waited with her basket, to be picked up to go to town. It always seemed to me that the sight of the memorial and the sight of the farm brought immense relief. From then on the journey sped up and could be endured. Many years, many countries and many homes later, I came back to live in that same farmhouse and still felt that same unspeakable relief when I caught sight of my

*More views of Anna Evans' grandmother's house in Pontrhydfendigaid.*

house and the tower.

There was a simplicity and robustness to country life then that seems to have all but vanished today. True country people were hardy, resourceful and tough. They had to be. There were few luxuries or refinements. Even as recently as the late 1970s a neighbour of mine had no tap water in the house; instead a tiny stream ran through the middle of his kitchen with the slate slabs cut to channel it. There was no electricity, no telephone, no indoor sanitation. The first thing this neighbour acquired when electricity was finally installed was a TV set, but that had to be taken with extension leads right up a field behind the house as that was the only spot with decent reception.

Although I usually only came back to Wales in the holidays, for some reason that I cannot now recall, I attended the little local school for a brief period of a week or two. This was a stone building standing next to the ruined Cistercian monastery of Strata Florida and it served as a schoolhouse to children from much of the outlying area. All the children were taught in the one room, graded only by age: younger at the front, older ones at the back. A large old stove stood to one side and every day each child brought an egg to school which the teacher cooked for them on the stove – same every day.

A summer came when I ventured the walk down from the house to play with the children from the Abbey farm. We had wonderful games romping and running all over the ruins, which in those days were largely hidden and buried under grassy mounds. We held tea parties, chased the geese, played hide and seek, paddled in the river and generally had a wonderfully free time. Now the little building that housed the schoolroom is a small museum. The grounds have been carefully excavated to preserve the remains of the twelfth-century abbey and many interesting discoveries have been unearthed. The grounds have been laid out as far as possible in the original form, right up to the boundary with the churchyard where members of my family, going back many years, are buried. The artefacts from the archaeological excavations have been carefully preserved, labelled and displayed behind glass and I find it amazing that anything remains from the onslaught of hordes of children who, like myself, over the centuries have chased and skipped and tumbled with little regard to what lay beneath.

Some of my most enduring memories are just little cameos, fragments out of time frozen forever in the mind. One is of Nana, hammering out Chopin on her Bechstein grand piano in the end drawing room, with all the doors and windows open. I sat on a step under a window where a japonica bush grew, listening, smiling when she got a note wrong and thumped all the harder. To this day I cannot hear Chopin pieces without being carried back to those warm, happy days. The japonica bush still grows there; alas, Nana and the piano have gone. I remember the sound of the wind rushing through the beeches and elms around the house, and the cries of the hundreds of rooks settling for the night; the almost unbearable sadness and stillness of a funeral at the little church for a farmer's wife and the memory of her red-haired young daughter, beside herself with grief. And I end where I began – Dick Jones.

Dick and his wife lived in a small terraced house in the village and were willing accomplices of my childhood schemes. I recall, when very young,

*Aberystwyth Football Club 1948/49. Mid Wales Football League champions. From left to right, back row: R.T. Jones (manager), Ron Cullum, Elfed Evans, Howard Williams, Evan Meredith, Elwyn Thomas, Gomer Thomas, Clem Phillips, Harry Feltham (trainer). Front row: Phil Andrews, Ivor James, Howell Simon, Ted Bevan, Eddie Ellis, Ted Thomas, John Ellis Williams.*

escaping to their house on more than one occasion and hiding under their table, to be retrieved by my mother or Nana. The Jones' kept a pig and the swill was stored in a churn in the passage at the side of the house. I loved to watch Mrs Jones adding scraps and peelings to it and stirring it, and later on Mr Jones taking it up to the field where the pig was kept. What a privilege to accompany him and watch from a safe distance as he fed it! The kindness and cheerfulness of that lovely couple still shines down the years, half a century later.

*Mrs A. Evans*

## The Old Black and Greens

Aberystwyth has always been a football town. If Aber were a nation – and I recall a former mayor, Sion Jobbins, likening it to an ancient Greek city-state – then football would undoubtedly be its national game. I mean, of course, association football or what the Americans like to call 'soccer', not rugby football, which has always seemed to me something of a foreign import in the town. (And let's be honest about this, the fanaticism over rugby in Wales is almost entirely confined to the South, leading to some gross misconceptions about the overall character of the Welsh.)

I grew up in Trefechan, just across the river from Park Avenue, Aber's very own Old Trafford or Delle Alpi. We could see the goal on the bus depot side and a fair portion of the pitch in that half from our front bedroom in Glanrafon Terrace, though not enough to make it worthwhile to sneak out of paying by viewing the match from there. My big brother Vic was a football fan, and my father was quite keen on the game too. Sadly, there wasn't much football locally, when I was growing up, as there was a war on. House matches in our junior school, Alexandra Road Boys' – I was in Dewi, naturally much better than Arthur, Padarn or Merlin – were played in Town Field (our name for Park Avenue) in practically knee-high grass. I remember my old pal Geraint Richards holding the cup aloft when Dewi won one year, and afterwards we all marched through the streets chanting rhetorically, ' Who said that Dewi couldn't play?' It was a slightly more pacific variant of 'Who said the turkey couldn't fly?', which was generally a prelude to battles with the 'foreigners' from across the river in Tan-y-Cae or even more distant parts of the town. ('Turkey', I should explain, was another name for Trefechan at that time; nobody quite knew why. Sadly it seems to have fallen out of use entirely now.)

Towards the end of the war, football began to reappear in the town. There was a match on Vicarage Field involving sturdy Aber veterans such as Albert 'the Fish' Davies and the butcher, 'Digger' Jones, whose well-rounded figures suggested that the dietary benefits of rationing had been much exaggerated. When competitions resumed, Aber – the 'Old Black and Greens' – fielded sides including George Christopher, a neighbour of ours at Glanrafon Terrace, and 'Jock' Donahue, a soldier who was billeted next door to us. Jock was a Glaswegian with an impenetrable accent. When I spoke to him over the privet hedge, in suitable awe at addressing so great a personage as an Aber first-team player, I was often reduced to nodding more or less intelligently in reply to his vociferous but totally baffling

*Rovers FC, 1952. From left to right, back row: Victor Williams (manager), Robert Bowen, John Howells, Ken Roscoe, Peter Meredith, Emlyn Edwards. Front row: David Jones, Gwyn Hughes, Islwyn Oliver, Ron Cullum, Henley Thomas, Peter Parry, Bill Lewis.*

*L.R. Roose Aberystwyth. Dr Leigh Richmond Roose played in goal for Aberystwyth from 1895 to 1900. He played twenty-four times for Wales, also played for Everton, Sunderland, Stoke and Glasgow Rangers as an amateur. He was a bacteriologist by profession.*

comments. Two of Aber's finest players in the post-war years, full-back Ted Bevan and inside-left Eddie Ellis, returned from the forces to prove storming successes. In the 1947/48 season, Eddie Ellis thumped in goals from all angles to prove he had lost none of the skills that had brought talent scouts from clubs like Arsenal to watch him as a schoolboy football prodigy. Ted Bevan was strong as an ox in defence and skippered the side in the big match of the season, against Barry in the Welsh Cup. We lost, but only just. The crowd was massive. Long afterwards I asked Ron Cullum, who played right-half that day, what the pre-match preparation had been. Were there long tactical talks? A secret plan? Ron smiled. 'No. Ted just picked up the ball, said 'do your best, lads' and out we went.'

Illness put me out of action as a spectator for two long years until I returned to an Aber on the brink of entering the Welsh League, Division Two (West). A huge step. They won promotion to Division One, and now the team had a bustling centre-forward in the old tradition, John Hughes Edwards – a Turkey boy – and a tricky inside-forward, John Ellis Williams, John 'Bach', who set up goals with a minimum of fuss. No footballer myself, I could merely admire and report their exploits in the Welsh Gazette, then rival to the Cambrian News, with offices in Bridge Street. It's one of my proudest boasts that I persuaded Ben Jones, the dour but thoroughly nice editor of the Gazette, to introduce a sports page with myself as a very young sports editor – no easy task, as he was an old-fashioned Cardiganshire Liberal who thought all sport a regrettable frivolity.

But football in Aber is much more than Aberystwyth FC. There have always been flourishing 'junior' clubs in the town and its hinterland – junior not in the sense of age but of status. The Aberystwyth and District League of that time was generally known as the Junior League and its secretary, Len Roberts, worked in a drapery store in Eastgate. There were fierce rivalries between the teams, who included Trefechan, Penparcau, Rovers, YMCA, Padarn United, Borth, Pontrhydfendigaid (Bont), Tregaron Turfs and Aberaeron. (No Penrhyncoch then, you will note.) Matches with Bont were sometimes of unbridled ferocity as they regularly fielded defenders who could take the legs off forwards trying any fancy stuff. No red and yellow cards then, and any referee rash enough to issue a warning to a Bont man on his home patch needed police protection.

Rovers – not Aberystwyth Rovers, just Rovers – were run by my brother Vic and his pals, notably Caradog Fisher Davies and Gary Lewis, known as 'Cooper' (Gary Cooper, geddit?). They had no ground of their own, thus the name Rovers. They fancied themselves a cut above the rest in football style and to prove it, their shirts were dead ringers for those of Wolverhampton Wanderers, then one of the top English League clubs (how times have changed). They could certainly play classy stuff and took a few trophies, though they were cut down to size at times by the terrible Turks. John 'Digger' Jones, son of the aforementioned veteran 'Digger' Jones, played fullback, Ron Cullum skippered their most successful sides and stalwarts included Tommy Masson, Geraint Roberts, Gwillam Lloyd Thomas, Wyn Hughes, Islwyn Fisher Davies, and my old pal Peter Parry. Forgive me, all those I've left out. I lost touch with Aber football in the sixties after moving to Cardiff but was aware of super players like Alan Blair, David Williams, Wil Lloyd, and Brian Pugh Jones in those black-and-green jerseys. This isn't an official history of Aberystwyth FC (or even an unofficial one), so I won't attempt to summarize the club's achievements since. Suffice to say the club is still there, the stadium looks better than ever, and when I come up to Aber you can often find me on Nark's Corner, next to John Hughes Edwards and Ron Cullum, who are as fervent supporters as they were players. As a paid-up Nark I find it sad that today, nobody plays for nothing – no wonder the club needs so much cash – and that players seem to switch clubs as often as they change their socks. Where is the pride in playing for Aber? Does it exist any more? It ought to, because Aberystwyth FC is one of the oldest clubs in Wales, and to play for

Town ought to be counted a privilege. Think of the players it has nurtured, not only in recent years but also in the distant past. The legendary Leigh Richmond Roose was reckoned to be a goalkeeping genius at the dawn of the twentieth century. Later came that famous halfback line of Sankey, Richards and Caul and the dynamic duo F.S. (Fred) Jones and 'Pop' Wright, Jones heading in goal after goal from the pinpoint crosses of left-winger Wright. No, I didn't see them – they were before even my time – but I've read about them in that excellent book, *The Old Black-and-Greens* by Peter Parry and Brian Lile. Shouldn't the players of today be proud to step into the footsteps of those giants, instead of quibbling over cash as if pocketing 'filthy lucre' were the only reason for kicking a ball?

But there, Narks – especially old Narks – shouldn't say too much. I'm proud that today's Aber is one of the most successful teams in the League of Wales, serving up football that's often a joy to watch. Thank you, players past and present, for giving me so much pleasure.

*Herbert Williams*

## Changes

I came to live in Wales just over thirty years ago and, in that fairly short time, I have seen many changes, particularly in the area in which I live. In the early days I used to drive an old convertible car, the top of which was always down. As long as one kept moving the rain would blow over the top. With no roof it was possible to carry an almost unlimited amount: ladders and tools for work and, for social events, the piano I had bought in the old salesrooms in

Aberystwyth for £6. On one occasion, two German hitch-hikers somehow managed to squeeze underneath it to shelter from the rain and entertained us later in the evening with a rather large number of drinking songs.

The first time I arrived in the village, the three old men who had been sitting on the bench opposite the shop all got up and came over, evidently a stranger was something of a rarity and an open car even more so. Starting with the usual question 'Bachgen, where are you from?', they inquired about the car. Was it thirsty? Was it very fast? What were the ladders for? and so on. At that time the village shop still sold petrol and I had just enough money to buy a gallon – 38 or 41p, I believe.

Like many other incomers to the area at that time, I managed to find an old farmhouse for rent. The first letter I had there was a receipt for half-yearly rates paid by the previous tenants – for the grand sum of £3.42! Keeping the Rayburn going was one of my main priorities in those days. The three open fires in the rest of the house, including one in the bedroom, were a luxury I could rarely afford. Coal itself was something of an extravagance at 50p a bag, so the main fuel was wood, and occasionally peat. When I enquired about peat I was told not to bother, that it was, 'a thing of the past' but when I brought the first load home, hardly any of the neighbours passed without stopping to advise me on the best place to get it, how to cut it – did I have a haearn mawn? – not to worry, they had an old one at home I could use. Likewise clogs were a thing of the past, but when I bought a second-hand pair in Carmarthen market for 50p, everyone told me how they remembered wearing them, how warm and comfortable they were, so

much better than Wellingtons, a pity no one wore them any more.

I was keen to learn Welsh, but knew that if I started to speak in English, people would reply in English and I wouldn't get any further. Fortunately I had friends who helped me with a few basic phrases, and by a process of trial and error and making a fool of myself quite often I'm sure, I gained a working knowledge of the language. Quite a bit of the work I did at that time was on local farms and, apart from painting and building work, I helped out with sowing barley, carrying hay and lifting potatoes, jobs which over the last few years have all disappeared.

I think that I did pretty well anything that turned up. I remember going out at night on an old Fordson Major tractor looking for stray ewes and taking them back to the farm; clearing out a yard with only a rhaw coes hir. I had never seen one before and had to be shown how to use it. The job took three days and I was paid £2; the farmer reasoned that as I had walked to and from his farm, had my meals there and, 'only gone home to sleep', I didn't really need the money, but could treat myself anyway.

On another occasion I was called out in the middle of a snowstorm to put slates back on a farmhouse roof. 'Snow is coming in the bedroom – you've got to come', I was told. The ladder was already in place; a rope went through an upstairs window and was securely lashed to the brass bedstead inside. I fixed the slates that were passed up to me out of the bedroom window, and then it was suggested that, ' while I was up there', I could perhaps sweep the chimney, a job that they'd been meaning to do for some time. Before I could reply, the farmer was crawling along the ridge tiles towards me with a bundle of rods and a chimney brush under one arm. I took the rods from him and, by stretching up, could just reach the top of the chimneystacks and peer inside. A huge mass of sticks, wool and waste paper completely blocked the opening. Laboriously I pulled it all out, and then inserted the brush and rods. After quite a long time, a small figure appeared from the house saying that the china cabinet in the parlour was moving; the rods had found a way through the stonework and were now poking through the wallpaper! No amount of pulling or pushing seemed to free them so, kneeling in the fireplace and cursing beneath his breath, the farmer actually managed to snap one of the rods, and pulled the rest down the chimney. The remaining ones were pushed back through the wallpaper and, as far as I know, are there to this day.

There have been extremes of weather: the August storm that washed away bridges overnight; the drought of '76, when few farms were on the mains and water for perhaps sixty or seventy cattle had to be carried in churns from the village tap. The stream at the bottom of the valley, which had been in flood for much of the previous winter, completely dried up. The fine weather gave a bumper hay crop and nearly every night for weeks there were hundreds of bales to be carried. Winter '81/82 was particularly severe, with huge drifts completely filling the lanes. Helicopters dropped supplies, and people walked miles across the fields for bread. At home, the fine flakes blew under the slates on the roof and covered everything in the loft with a foot of snow, so cold that it did not thaw for over a week; and in a neighbour's house, water froze in a glass on the kitchen table.

Over the years the pattern of things has changed quite a bit: thirty years ago, working on Sunday was unheard of. I was given quite a telling off for saying that I was to fix my car at the weekend. 'Not on a Sunday, bachgen!' Hay has given way to silage, dom to slurry, tractors have suspension, sound systems and heated cabs – a far cry from the old Fergie bach! Most of the old characters I knew when I first moved here have gone, in turn remembered by fewer and fewer people. Looking back, it seems that I just caught a glimpse of the old way of things in the country. In coming to Wales I saw places, met people and made friends that I will never forget.

*J.J. Danks*

## Uncle Tommy's Pierrots

'...So if you want to have a jolly good time, Come round Aber with me.'
So ran the last two lines of the opening song, sung by the full company of Uncle Tommy's 1939 troupe. They wore black and orange lozenge harlequin costumes; the uncles in those innocent days, black faced, after the style of Al Jolson. The aunties' ballerina-style costumes were designed to show off their legs. Uncle Tommy's Castle Showground Troupe was beginning another evening's entertainment. The adults sat in deck chairs, while we children crowded onto forms at the very front. In spite of Uncle Tommy's exhortations, more people enjoyed the show outside the ground than actually sat in it. These freeloaders vanished like the tide going out on South Beach when the collectors arrived with their collecting boxes and, like that tide, came back when the collectors returned to the stage door.

In those pre-war days we were easily diverted and entertained. Slapstick still ruled the sketches. Uncle Tommy, when not

*Pierrots at Aberystwyth Castle.*

playing the drums compèred the show, introducing the 'Uncles' and 'Aunties' in turn to the audience. There was a kilted and sporraned Scots comedian who did a Will Fyffe routine ending with 'I belong in Glasgow', the audience joining in heartily. Auntie Shirley bewitched us with her dance routines. Another 'Uncle', playing the banjo or ukulele, sang some of George Formby's more risqué numbers. This caused us, the juvenile urchins of the town, to nudge each other, giggle and force the child sitting on the end of the row to fall off, so causing a further outburst of barely suppressed hysteria. There were two acts though, which were anathema to us. We sat restlessly, shuffled and talked throughout Uncle George's spot. Uncle George, a pianist, sang such heavyweight numbers as, 'Old Man River', 'On the Road to Mandalay' and a lugubrious Edwardian song 'Friend of Mine'. However, the mass exodus of juveniles occurred when Aunty Doris swept onto the stage. Poor Aunty Doris! Big bosomed and evening-gowned, trailing a voile scarf, she launched into light opera numbers or one of Ivor Novello's more popular hits while we decamped en masse, in spite of Uncle Tommy's threats and best efforts to detain us. Off we went to the toilets or to buy Bitchell's penny ice cream cornets. We returned in anticipation of the children's 'Go As You Please' talent competition.

As he declaimed: 'Some of the biggest names in entertainment began as children on such a stage as this. George Robey, Vesta Tilley, even Sir Henry Irving himself!' We erupted onto the stage to sing the 'Ovalteenies' song:
'We are the Ovalteenies, happy girls and boys,
Make your request we'll not refuse you,

We are here just to amuse you…'
Then one by one we would be introduced to the audience. My friend Henley inevitably sang a wistful number, 'When I grow too old to dream' while I, a choirboy in St Michael's church, had an eclectic repertoire of totally unsuitable hymns. One was a melancholy Lenten dirge:
'Christian dost thou see them on the holy ground.
How the troops of Midian prowl and prowl around'.
But I came to grief once, when I overreached myself wildly by single-handedly attempting Handel's 'Hallelujah Chorus', much to the total hilarity of the audience, when I forgot the words halfway through. The winner was the child who received the largest show of hands and went on to Friday night's All Winners grand finale. Inevitably, the winner was the child who had most relations in the audience or a fearsome dad who glared threateningly at anyone daring not to vote for his child. The highlight of the Pierrot season was the ten o'clock 'Midnight Matinée' held usually in August.

In 1939, that last summer of peace, there was something very nostalgic about songs drifting down from the Castle grounds to the crowded promenade below and, yes, Aber was crowded in those days! 'When the deep purple falls over sleepy garden walls' created a feeling of melancholy in the listeners as they passed Castle Point. The winds were warm and soft off the sea; tomorrow was another holiday day on the beach. Like so many more at that time, and young as I was, I too hoped it would go on forever. Sadly, for all of us, we had but a few more weeks to go before the world, as we knew it, ended.

*Richard Emlyn Edwards*

27

*Ice cream and oysters on the pier.*

*Alexandra Road showing the station in the 1900s.*

## My Home Town

In the 1930s, with the bad old days of the Depression over, Aberystwyth was once again becoming a thriving little seaside resort with its hotels and boarding houses full of visitors, predominantly Midlanders enjoying their annual week or two-week holidays.

Every weekend the railway station, newly painted with its beautiful hanging baskets of flowers and clean, well-swept platforms would be a hive of activity. There were porters a-plenty, all anxious to help the travellers with their luggage and always hopeful of a few coppers' tip. Often the stationmaster (Mr Collins) could be seen in his smart uniform with its gold braid, looking very much in authority. Outside the station, the long hand trucks and porters from the seafront hotels (the name of the hotel painted on the side: Belle Vue,

Marine, Queen's etc.) all waiting to transport the luggage of their guests to their respective hotels. It was very easy to distinguish between those who were arriving and those who were leaving from their unmistakable sun-tan, or lack of it; it was a fact that Aberystwyth boasted some of the highest recorded daily hours of sunshine in the whole country and the publicity department of the town was not slow to take advantage of the fact. Placards and hoardings in all the main GWR and LMS stations such as Snow Hill (Birmingham), Paddington (London) and Piccadilly (Manchester) invited people to spend their holidays in 'Aberystwyth, the place in the sun where the mountains come down to the sea'.

Aberystwyth's claim to be the 'Biarritz of Wales' was perfectly justified and its significance as a major holiday resort was acknowledged countrywide. So important

*On board pleasure boat, c. 1935.*

*Lifeboat on Aberystwyth beach.*

did the great railway companies regard it, that several express trains a day ran to and from the major cities of England and Wales, from as far afield as London and the West of England. It is interesting to note that the journey from Aberystwyth to London could be undertaken in less than six hours – a time that, even at the present day, has never been bettered.

Despite the fact that the town could not boast the fine golden sands of Borth or other places along the coast, the seafront at Aberystwyth never the less had plenty to offer its visitors in the way of attractions and entertainment. Central to these was the promenade with its fine Victorian pier stretching out into the sea with the Pier cinema its centrepiece, and the formidable figure of Sergeant Major Mathias, with his military bearing and beefeater moustache, standing in the entrance as commissionaire. Overlooking Marine

Terrace was the Pier Café with its hanging vines and colourful flower baskets.

Beyond the pavilion, at its seaward extremity, a couple of buildings with pagoda-type roofs, one of which was an aviary. Every August bank holiday, as part of the aquatic sports, Albert Davies ('the Fish') would jump into the sea from here, dressed in women's clothes and holding an open parasol, then riding a surf board with young Myfanwy Hughes on his shoulders. A group of local lads, all good swimmers, known as the 'Human Seals', took part in various aquatic events and displays such as pillow fighting on a greasy pole to win the prize of a joint of ham which hung at the end. Numerous life-saving, swimming and diving competitions were held, all the events culminating at six o'clock in the firing of the lifeboat maroons and the launching of the lifeboat, which had been on the promenade all day on exhibition to the public. Sadly at least half of the pier was destroyed in the great storm of January 1938, never to be rebuilt.

On the promenade outside the pier, were the two Paddies in clean white aprons, their cart full of fresh Whitstable oysters, whelks and cockles. A little further on was Freddie Kenyon, his cart piled high with fresh fruit, laid out with great care to tempt the passer-by; then, at intervals all along the promenade were the ice-cream vendors with their trucks and tricycles: names such as Antoniazzi, Davies the Lorne and Bitchell, selling cornets at a penny and wafers at twopence or threepence.

After breakfast every fine summer day, Jack Price and the faithful John Bach would bring their donkeys to the promenade and all day long these lovely animals, some saddled and others pulling donkey carts, would give rides to delighted children up and down the well-trodden road from the donkey stand to the pier and back. The donkeys were so accustomed to this routine that when they reached the turning point, without even a word from their handlers they would turn around and return to their starting point. Each donkey had its own name written on the bridle across its forehead, such colourful names as Blossom, Rosey, Beauty etc. During the local carnival week, a donkey derby would be held and the spectators, parents and children, would call out these names, spurring on the animal of their choice.

Further to the north of the donkey stand, drawn up in a line, were the charabancs of the Jones brothers and Benny Price, with their placard boards offering the visitor a day or half-day's outing to places of interest and scenic beauty in the surrounding countryside.

Another focal point on this part of the promenade was of course the bandstand. Until the mid-1930s this was a wooden structure built on piles, then in 1935, to commemorate

*Fleet visit in 1925.*

the Silver Jubilee of King George V, a new circular concrete bandstand was built, designed by the then borough surveyor, Llewelyn Jones. It was said to be one of the prettiest in Wales. Unfortunately it proved not to be completely practical and some years later it was redesigned to give the public more protection from the elements. Over the years it has provided a place of entertainment and much pleasure to numerous visitors and local people: bands and orchestras, Pierrots and singers, and in more recent years national radio roadshows. What a delight it was in summers gone by, on a fine sunny afternoon or evening, to see hundreds of deck-chairs full of people across the promenade from the bandstand to the roadside and Will Nell, his head buried under the black sheet of his plate camera, taking the sepia holiday snaps, mementos of happy times. On the beach just to the north of the bandstand, the dozen or so green canvas bathing tents stood in line like sentry boxes, and in front of them the Whoopee-floats, hired out at a shilling an hour: small, twin-hulled floats on which the bather sat and propelled himself with a paddle.

No description of Aberystwyth's seafront of this era would be complete without including the pleasure boats of which there were quite a number, of varying size. There were rowing boats licensed to carry six or eight people with their own boatman, offering hour-long trips at the cost of a shilling each; and then there were the bigger motor boats, namely the *Belle-Isle*, *Swanee*, *King George*, *Skylark*, *Sea Hawk*, *Emerald Star* etc., which operated from either side of the life-boat slipway and made two-hour mackerel fishing trips from six o'clock in the morning until late in the evening. The boat supplied all fishing tackle, and each boat carried a crew of two. The fare for such a trip was a half a crown. On completion of each trip a familiar sight was that of the disembarking passengers carrying their strings of fresh

mackerel and the boxes of surplus fish being sold to the public at the top of the lifeboat slipway.

Along the beach, opposite the bandstand, the larger motor boats, *Wild Rose*, *County of Warwick*, *Pride of the Midlands* and the *Worcester Castle*, with their long gangways onto the beach, took people for half-hour trips around the bay at a price of one shilling, children half-price of course. At the height of the season the *Pride* and the *Worcester*, which were much larger than the other boats, ran an afternoon trip to Aberdovey leaving at 2.15 p.m. with two hours ashore, returning at 6 p.m.; the fare was five shillings. At the end of each working day when the boats were returning to the harbour for the night, it was customary to give the children who had been playing on the beach a free trip to the harbour. The names of the boatmen who ran these pleasure-boats will long be remembered, not only because of the boats, but in very many cases for their service in the Aberystwyth lifeboats, the crews of which were drawn from these professional seamen.

One event, which took place annually before the war and less frequently in the few years after it, was the visit of Royal Navy warships. These ships would anchor some two or three miles off in the bay for a few days to a week at a time, during which time all sorts of civil and social functions would be held in their honour including a Mayor's banquet for the senior officers and various dances. The ships would of course reciprocate by entertaining the town's dignitaries with a cocktail party and opening the ship to the public every afternoon from 2 p.m. to 6 p.m. At night these ships would be lit up and on the final night of their visit an impressive searchlight display was staged. The visits of these ships, as one would imagine, attracted even more people to the town to the benefit of business people and local boatmen. There were also a lot of assignations, the young ladies of the town and countryside taking full advantage of this influx of eligible young men; in more than one case this resulted in an addition to the town's population!

In Marine Terrace was the King's Hall, built as the Municipal Hall at the cost of some £21,000 and later renamed; it was opened in 1934. During its lifetime it was a theatre, dance hall, conference hall and exhibition hall. In its early life the open-air roof garden was very popular with summer visitors and an ideal vantage point from which to view whichever event was taking place on the promenade below. For me, and I have no doubt for a good many others, the King's Hall clock is sadly missed, despite the fact that on some occasions it stopped. I think that on the whole it was a great asset and doubtless a good many day-trippers, enjoying themselves on the sea-front, were glad of its presence when having to rush for their bus or train home. As a theatre and concert hall, the building billed many famous national and international stars. Names that come to mind are the Bachelors, the Rolling Stones, Cyril Stapleton, and the London Symphony and Philharmonic orchestras. Apart from these there were of course a lot of local shows put on by amateur dramatics societies and concert troupes. One particular annual event, which drew full houses, was the Ardwyn production of Gilbert and Sullivan operas. With its spacious dance-floor (the biggest in town), the mid-week and Saturday night dances especially were a great success: dancing to the music of Everard Davies and his band, all of who were local musicians. Ronnie Hughes, the trumpet player, was later to have a very successful career in some of the most famous dance bands in the country. The band's female vocalist, Pegi Edwards, was often heard on the BBC. During the war years, the King's Hall dances were especially popular with the thousands of servicemen and women who were stationed in the town.

Another popular attraction, in the basement of the King's Hall, was Tuson's Amusements with its rifle ranges, slot machines and large bumping boat-lake in the centre (this was later converted to bumper-cars). During the war years this basement was also used by the Royal Air Force Training Wing to hold boxing matches. One famous British boxing champion, who gave exhibition fights at these bouts, was Freddie Mills. After the war the basement amusements were run by Messrs Day and Sons who continued until the demolition of the building in 1989.

Before moving on from this part of the town, its history would not be complete without a mention of the custom of kicking the Bar. The bar is the low railing at the northern most end of the promenade (Victoria Terrace, opposite Alexandra Hall) and it was the custom of the local people and students to kick this bar with their foot before turning to retrace their steps, having walked the length of the promenade.

*Desmond Davies*

## Aberystwyth in the Thirties and Forties

The first thing I remember was the sea and the seagulls – thank goodness they're there still – thunderous roaring, loud screeching and the wind slapping against my face. I think this was after some great storm when my father had taken my older sister and me down to inspect the damage. I cried and wanted to go home to the Waun where the elements were altogether less ferocious.

I wasn't very happy about a return visit to the town, but it proved completely different,

*Donkey rides on the prom.*

a rare afternoon of mild blue skies and docile sea. And donkeys. Oh, the dear, patient, plodding donkeys on the prom, some grey, some brown, real eyes with eyelashes, fluffy round tummies, wispy tails, I knew that if I could have one of my own I would be happy for ever and ever, but my mother was adamant that it was quite impossible: they belonged to the mayor and mayoress of Aberystwyth and I was a very lucky girl to be allowed to ride on one, and please choose quickly because they were waiting to be off.

When you were three years old, all fringe, big eyes and frilly dress, the boy in charge took your donkey's reins and you rode in front of all the rest and it was the best time of your life, with the salty smell of the sea and everyone looking at you and you feeling like Shirley Temple or Princess Margaret Rose.

When you were four and there were smaller, daintier girls, one of those little

creeps was chosen to lead, and you had to ride behind with the rest of the mob. It was a devastating lesson about Time's cruelty. I peaked at three.

Never mind, a donkey ride was still better than anything else in the world, far preferable to ice cream, crisps or Milky Ways that were the other things you could get for tuppence, the extent of my spending power.

One unforgettable afternoon, an acquaintance of my mother's, seeing me still hanging about the donkeys long after my ride was over, offered me money for another. 'She's had a turn,' my mother said. 'Well, let her have a second,' said this munificent woman – who wasn't even an auntie – lifting me up onto the nearest donkey's back. On such moments we catch dim glimpses of the Kingdom of Heaven.

I was never very fond of the sea; it was too sudden and splashy, and to reach it required too much painful hobbling over sharp pebbles. Other more fortunate children had little rubber slip-on shoes for the beach, but my mother considered that stumbling over stones toughened the soles of our feet. And probably our souls too. She was a daughter of the Manse. Another thing I failed to appreciate was sand in my knickers. To tell you the truth, I preferred picnics in a field, safely home in the Waun.

The Waun was a very quiet hamlet where everyone knew everyone else, one long road with a Methodist chapel, a shop called Hendre stores, but always referred to as 'The Shop' as there was no other, three farms and a letter-box. Before the war cars were rare. When I was very little I used, occasionally, to go with my older sister to the main road, the top of Penglais – an ordinary country road in those days – to write down the registration numbers of passing cars. Neither she nor I was particularly enamoured of this pastime, but we knew that it was something that other, older children, did. I think that there was only one car actually owned by

a Waun inhabitant. It was a big grey two-seater driven by a man called Mr Milton. I seem to remember that he had a beard as well. Also, he was English. Welsh people seemed to make do with a motorbike and sidecar. Miss Milton, sister of the car-owning Mr Milton, was very tall and stately. They lived in what might have been a mansion. (But to be honest any house with a bathroom, a garage and more than three bedrooms was called a mansion in our society.) You went to Miss Milton first when collecting for the Missionary Society – y Genhadaeth – because she gave you sixpence when everyone else gave you pennies. If you collected fifteen shillings you got a book, too boring to read but all the same, much prized. I'm often surprised, and indeed rather alarmed, to realize that my efforts helped to spread Christianity to places like India and China that seem to have perfectly good religions of their own. Whenever Mormons call on me, I find myself wondering if their little children back in

*Bandstand built to celebrate the Silver Jubilee of George V, 1935.*

Utah are making door-to-door collections for my salvation. Quite a sweet thought.

In the thirties, everyone went to church or chapel. We went to Soar Congregational Chapel in Llanbadarn. When I was very little, I only went to Sunday school and when it was raining or very cold, I was allowed to go to the Methodist Sunday school on the Waun. In Llanbadarn we learnt that good children went on the Sunday school trip and had a present from the Christmas tree, and naughty children went on the big fire – y Tan Mawr. No contest really! The lavatory was the most exciting thing about Soar; a long seat with three holes for different sizes of bottom, over an earth pit. It had probably been there since the chapel was rebuilt in the nineteenth century, when it was the last word in modernity, and certainly more sheltered than the bushes behind the chapel.

In the Waun, we recited from a catechism called Rhodd Mam (Mother's Gift). I learnt from this that God made me. (And I wondered crossly why He had chosen to make me with straight, brown hair and Eirlys Jones with honey-coloured curls.) All the same, I did marginally prefer going there because it was the Sunday school my sweetheart, Tom Williams, attended, and once in a while he would deign to talk to me.

On weekdays I went to Cwmpadarn Elementary School in Llanbadarn where my father, Percy Davies, was the headmaster. When I was in his class, he was stricter with me than anyone else, always very angry when I wasted time dreaming or chattering. Before I sat the scholarship exam, he warned me not to choose the story option because I'd get carried away and would fail to finish, so I wouldn't get the excellent marks I

needed to make up for my sloppy handwriting and somewhat original spelling. His influence on my literary style was immense. It was wartime so we weren't allowed to waste a scrap of paper on unnecessary words. And I've been saving paper ever since. It means I'll never write a popular blockbuster, but on the other hand, I won't bore people with long, superfluous purple passages.

After elementary school, I went to Ardwyn, which I don't hold in such high esteem as most other people. I certainly passed exams while I was there, but don't feel that my particular needs were satisfied. Most old pupils seem to enthuse about the Gilbert and Sullivan operas that took so much of our time during the autumn term and were performed for three nights at the end of that term. For me, they were a complete waste of time because I could neither sing nor dance. My uncle was a teacher at Machynlleth Grammar School and there they performed an annual Shakespeare play. At the beginning of my second year at school – and abetted by my father – I went to the Head's study, asking whether it would be possible for the school to perform a Shakespeare play on alternate years; or even occasionally. He seemed stunned by my temerity in making such an irreverent suggestion. 'We'd never raise the same amount of money,' he spluttered, showing that profit, even then, was the most important consideration. I'm sure that many others must have yearned, as I did, for the opportunity to take part in a classical play, but it never came.

I can't remember any theatre company coming to Aberystwyth. My mother could remember Lewis Casson and Sybil Thorndyke bringing their *Macbeth* to the town, but I was too young to attend that. In the fifties, there was a summer repertory theatre in Bath Street with Edna Dore – still going strong – leading the company. During my schooldays though there was only one cinema. The Pier cinema had closed at the beginning of the war, but we still had the Coliseum and the Forum. The back row of the Coliseum was the favoured Saturday night haunt of my generation whatever film was showing, as it was where we practised kissing and snogging and what is now termed heavy petting. I remember one film particularly. It was called *The Travels of Marco Polo* and especially memorable because I managed to see only the last reel, superb mountain scenery and a voice saying, 'Sir, it is called Cathay.' I enjoyed that film very much, but I'm sorry to admit that I can't now remember whom I was enjoying it with.

In high summer, seeking the same pleasures, we went up to the golf links. A character in one of my early novels says, 'If God hadn't intended us to make love out of doors, He wouldn't have invented bracken.' Aberystwyth people of my age would certainly be able to relate to that. Though perhaps I should add that most teenagers at that time didn't 'go all the way'. Getting to that place was altogether too dangerous. But the part of the way we did go was extremely worthwhile and exciting.

What did the war mean to a person of my generation? I remember food shortages and the strange taste of margarine, but I don't think we were too badly affected. My father, like most local men I suppose, grew plenty of fruit and vegetables, so there was always something to eat. I remember going to an Urdd camp in Llangranog though, and the only thing we could buy without

coupons or points, was tomato ketchup. So that was the only thing we had for our midnight feasts, on the slices of bread we managed to smuggle out of the canteen under our shirts.

I remember having to take a gas mask to the elementary school once a week at the beginning of the war – and having to miss playtime on those Mondays when I forgot it. I remember the influx of evacuees from Liverpool who seemed so sophisticated and spoke a form of English I couldn't understand. For a short period we had school only in the morning, so that they could be there in the afternoon, but of course, that was too good to last. Many of them returned, and the ones who remained had school in the church hall with their own teacher. We had a mother and baby staying with us: Mrs Hart and David who was eighteen months old and whom I loved even more than my own family.

When I was older, I was often nervous of the bombing we heard about on the news, and had frequent nightmares. My brother was in the Intelligence Corps in Burma, and of course the whole family worried about him.

From time to time at assembly in Ardwyn, the Head read out the name of a previous student who had been reported killed or missing and I was aware that one day my brother's name could be on the list. For me, the worst thing happened in 1944 when Belsen was liberated and pictures of the survivors were shown in the newspapers and on the *Pathé Gazette* news. I've never been able to forget the horror of those pictures. I was old enough by this time to experience the full force of the tragedy, including that terrible picture of the huge pile of children's shoes that had

*From left to right: Mrs Evans Driud, Mrs Bejamin Tanyrochor, Mrs Evans Claylands, Morfudd Evans, Valery Evans.*

not yet been salvaged from the camp.

I remember the excitement of VE Day with parties and a fancy dress parade through the town. For me, and for most other people, VJ Day was far more sombre though, because of the atom bomb that had precipitated it, the pictures of the countless people who had been liquidated by the blast.

These are some of my memories, good and bad.

*Sian James*

## The Summer of the Aeroplane

Throughout each summer, I lived with my grandmother alongside the London road. This, before it grew into the A44, smelled of hot tar and horse-dung rather than petrol. Traffic was so infrequent that we could lie out our mats on the road for their weekly brushing. The baker's van called on Tuesdays and Fridays and Mr Clark from Ponterwyd brought greengrocery each Thursday. We measured our time by the four daily buses as often as by the clock, and a

Sunday school trip to Shrewsbury was an expedition. It was a very static life, without electricity or running water, pedestrian in more than one sense.

Then, literally from a clear sky, Modern Technology, like a gigantic and angry wasp, flew down the valley, circled twice and landed tidily on top of Scwlfa, right above us. An aeroplane, a real live aeroplane, here!

I was mad with excitement but Mamgu said, calmly, 'That'll be Ioan Bebb, Blaendyffryn.' and went on picking beans. I was still open-mouthed in the front garden when all the children in Goginan came roaring up the road and Rona Davies kindly scooped me into the crowd. We raced up the steep face of the mountain and watched Ioan Bebb direct his helpers as they wheeled the tiny plane into a safer position. There was so little flat space on top of Scwlfa; it must have required a considerable skill to be able to land her, and even more to relaunch her. All children were firmly warned away, far away from the machine. We didn't resent this; even to our inexperienced eyes the plane looked too fragile to carry its two passengers.

Our elders followed us, but only when they'd changed into their 'going-out' clothes. Women climbed up through the bracken in tight shoes and long, crepe-de-chine dresses. I remember seeing one fox-fur, and hats were almost obligatory. In an old photograph, five of us stand proudly beside the wings. Mrs Evans the Druid and Mrs Evans Claylands are decently hatted and even Mamgu is without her usual apron. Obviously she felt that the Event was too

*Robin Goodfellow's Flying Flea, 1932.*

local to merit her hat. Valmai Evans and I are well combed and scrubbed.

Everyone wanted to see the plane. People walked from miles around. So many in fact, that Ioan became worried that some idiot might, one night, try to fly. He organized a volunteer guard.

Before the First World War few had seen an aeroplane, let alone taken a flight, but in the twenties groups of ex-pilots, mostly from the Royal Flying Corps, formed Flying Circuses, set up in any convenient field, where enthusiastic crowds would pay to watch aerial acrobatics or to take daring and expensive 'flips'. Alan Cobham was the most famous aviator (in London our cat was named after him) and Ioan Bebb flew for Cobham's Circus. To be so near one of Cobham's planes was to touch fame. Most of us were content to admire from a distance, but some of the young and reckless bought trips over Aberystwyth and the sea. Bebb subjected the more boastful to quite spectacular acrobatics and the effect on certain digestions became legendary. That aeroplane made our summer.

But this was in 1935 and in a few years, Ioan Bebb himself became a legend. His name is in the RAF Book of Honour in the crypt of St Paul's, near Nelson's tomb. He is listed as John Bebb and there is no mention of Blaendyffryn.

*Morfudd Bernard*

## The Seventies: A Time of Change

I came to Aberystwyth towards the end of the seventies. The government, under Jim Callaghan, was in pitched battle with the unions. Rubbish, refused by bin-men, piled up in the streets, capping a series of strikes by various sectors of the workforce. The unions were holding the country to ransom, complained the newspapers. The economy was not competitive, warned the increasingly confident Tories. The elections arrived. Saatchi and Saatchi came up with that unforgettable slogan: 'Labour isn't working'.

Callaghan soundly beaten, we found ourselves unknowingly on the eve of perhaps the biggest social and cultural change in twentieth-century Britain, under an unexpected, virtually unknown woman Prime Minister. It was the end of the controlled economy, the beginning of the free market and its forces. 'Socialism' was to become a dirty word, 'Keynesianism' an anachronism, like all other 'isms'. But it hadn't quite started happening. Idealists still had voices, and in Aberystwyth – which has still only ever once voted for a main party candidate – these were not socialist voices.

Aberystwyth was the centre of the Welsh language movement, the Welsh Language Society occupying a dingy office in an out-of-the-way basement in Albert Street. This office is one of the things I remember, even though I was never in it. We all recall different things, peculiar to ourselves, which brings me to admit that what I write is just my view, but how else does one look back at the changing life of a place? The mind surveys a period of time and a few things step forward, various, unconnected. You connect them. Do you then have history? Who would want to deny it its question mark?

So what do I recollect? Well, the political flavour of the Black Lion in Bridge Street; a detective called Ted Nicholas dreaming he was incognito in his plain clothes; Operation Fire; Che Guevara on people's walls, and of all things a short craze for

Citizen's Band radio. In the eighties I recall the rally in support of the miners' strike and later, in the nineties, the Queen's aborted visit.

There was something refreshingly cosmopolitan about moving to a holiday resort – I could be more anonymous in Aberystwyth than in homely Blaenau Ffestiniog, where I was approached on arrival and asked who I was and why I was there. One of the first things I noticed about Aberystwyth was the amount of English spoken on the street. There was a lot of English, compared with Blaenau, in the seventies. By the end of the nineties you had begun to notice it when Welsh was spoken on the streets of Aberystwyth. The language has declined. It is the second time I've lived through this phenomenon, the first time in my hometown of Llanelli, where Welsh seemed to disappear from under my very nose.

Back in the seventies, in Aberystwyth, the language was not just strong, it was a political force. This was just a decade from the explosive protests that had accompanied the flooding of Tryweryn, the bombs that had exploded during the Investiture in 1969 and John Jenkins bombing water pipes all over Wales. The famous occupation of Trefechan Bridge, the first protest by the newly formed Welsh Language Society, had taken place in 1962 and protesters who had been young then were protesting all the more effectively in the seventies, often from respected, even esteemed social positions.

The language was literally a burning issue. The Black Lion was full of colourful, quasi-political, local reprobates, who managed to have a very good time, and students, who sang 'We'll Burn Your Houses Down' to the tune of 'Those Were the Days'. The television series *Alas Smith and Jones* cracked

its famous joke: 'Come home to a real fire, buy a holiday cottage in Wales.' The shadowy Mydiad Amdiffyn Cymru, known as MAC, was getting away with arson. The Establishment struck back with Operation Fire. Chief Inspector Pat Malloy (now a local Welsh historian worth reading on Carmarthen town) cast a wide net, arresting, holding and releasing forty-eight, mainly middle-class Welsh citizens, many from Aberystwyth and its environs.

A senior lecturer at the university and a librarian blacked out television reception from Blaen Plwyf, just outside Aberystwyth, in protest against the lack of Welsh. Over 1,500 people from all over Wales refused to pay their television licences, forcing the government to concede over the issue of S4C. And one day Caio Evans, erstwhile General of the Free Welsh Army, rode down Terrace Road on a horse, dressed as a cowboy. It was all such a long time ago.

In those days the King's Hall, with bumper cars in its basement, stood where balconied flats gaze out to sea today. You could catch mackerel on the beach with just a bucket. The wooden jetty wasn't built, nor the new sewage works, and the harbour smelled at times. There were mud flats where the marina is. You could walk to the end of the pier. Large stores have replaced the coal yard. The Halls of Residence were half the size they have recently become and Alexander Hall was occupied, where today it has fallen into ruin. Parc-y-Llyn did not exist. There was no student village. The university had no intention of going into business. It had a fraction of the students it now attracts. It was a quieter town, especially at weekends. No one would have thought of turning a chapel into a pub. There were no beggars on the streets. It seems almost like another century. 'Global' was a word unuttered in relation to economics, culture or society. Views of society were more microscopic than telescopic, the buzzword then being 'community', in the sense that had to do with a district. I worked in what was thought of for a while as a 'Community College'.

Looking back, the peaceful protests of the Welsh Language Society and the clandestine burning of holiday cottages by MAC coincide with a more general turning point in society. They mark the end of a period when life was slower, when communities mattered more than profits, days when villagers left their doors open and individuals committed themselves to social issues. Those burnings mark the end of a time when it could be considered wrong for someone to want more than one house at the expense of someone else's community, to want an empty house just to have holidays, while local people searched for a roof over their heads, priced out of the market. Today the market is the only measure.

We are remote from those old days, from that kind of thinking, and of course we have reaped material rewards from the new, market economy. Suffice to say that there is no turning back the clock – that those times are history. Let us record, then, if only for those too young to remember them, what produced those past times, and what the purpose was. It was quite simply this. The economy was seen as something to be controlled for the benefit of society, and that was the job of politicians. Today, they collect and spend our taxes and we wonder why we need so many of them, but in those days the government was the country's largest employer. Maybe at the expense of some efficiency the government provided job security, and legislated to protect it,

which kept communities intact. Communities had expectations of their citizens and by serving their community people felt they mattered, which brought them commitment and character. Looking back, one could say that in those days the purpose was to try to operate a social ideal, yet it did work, even if imperfectly. That was the system, from the end of the Second World War till the end of the seventies.

I don't know why Citizen Band radio, a brief American import, sticks in my mind as it does. Maybe because it was just that – brief and American, a tiny flash-forward to what was to come. There were, of course, no mobile phones then. The excitement lay in talking on the move, talking American. An Aberystwyth youth driving through Llanon arranges to meet a friend from Aberaeron:

'Got your ears on?'

'Hello Skyscraper. Gimme a twenty.'

'Double L heading for Atlantis. Where's your twenty?'

'Boot Hill on square wheels.'

'How about an eyeball, big buddy?'

'Ok. See you on top of the world. 10.10.'

It was fast and slick, with no need to think. You bought a book of the code and a pamphlet re-naming your vicinity's place names and slipped into your new quasi-American identity. Within a couple of years the Prime Minister, Mrs Thatcher, would herself deploy American idioms, breaking with custom. We had been borrowing Americanisms, especially slang, since the thirties, when the cinema got big. We bulk borrowed in the sixties. But the Establishment didn't. It never approved, let alone did it itself. The Establishment stuck to the 'old boy' slang of the English public school system. It was in the Thatcher years that this began to go. So I see Citizen Band radio as the unrecognized clue to what was coming.

Who, after all, do we imitate? We imitate those with power and those whom the powerful admire, and these were not going to be public school heroes or idealistic left-wing reformers any more, or new playwrights or innovative young singer/song writers. They were going to be the people in *Hello* magazine. Our newspapers' pages were going to be dedicated to what had hitherto been called trivia, renamed glamour. A powerful American consumer culture was coming, calling itself 'global', because it had designs on the world. The empire couldn't strike back, so it was quick to join up – that is how the 'Great' was going to be put back in 'Britain', as we were promised. What was there to withstand it, in a Britain whose cultures had been always subordinated to the 'High Culture' of its ruling class? The young CB enthusiast's own culture had never been valued. And what did the old fashioned Establishment have to fight back with? Ascot? The Henley Regatta? The changing of the guards? Medals of the British Empire?

The Britain of the eighties had a choice of two allegiances, two models within the emerging global economy. There was Europe, and compromise with the unions, which in Europe continued to have their say, or there was the more extremely capitalist America. Britain chose America. Soon employers were able to fire at will, employ on short-term contracts and rely on disposable part-time labour. At the same time leisure became expensive, as what you owned and wore mattered more and style became more important. Global entertainment was to become the commercial province of an American culture with a surprising lack of censorship, poor public education and an astonishing crime level. However, on the plus side, the English language as a social indicator – snob value in the way you talked in Britain – would start counting for less, at last, because imitating the old ruling class would lose significance.

Rearguard action on behalf of the Queen's English continued, of course, and no doubt will be fought to the last ditch. Notably, though, while the Queen's accent hasn't changed, her Christmas address to the nation is nothing like the same as it was. The word 'service' was long ago dropped from the Queen's speech, for sounding paternalistic and class-ridden, while at the same time our new society dropped the old morality of contribution and co-operation. How a word can change! 'Service' now denotes our main industry.

I for one am sorry the Queen was pelted with eggs on Penglais Hill in 1996, not only because no one should be pelted, but because she was no longer a valid symbol of power in the new meritocracy, in which citizens compete for what they can get, contributing little voluntarily. In the real America you don't even give an after-dinner speech for free. That's the true ethos of the 'global village', the ethos of an economic system in which power leaves the hands of governments for the hands of global corporations. The dream is that these multinationals will do better than governments, that there will be more peace in the world. It's a dream rather like policeman Ted's about his plain clothes. Everyone saw through him, as everyone sees through big business's concern for world peace and the common good. What was it Tacitus said in the *Agricola* about the Romans going into Scotland? 'They create a desert and call it peace.'

When Citizen Band radio strutted its

brief hour in 1981, its real signals went unrecognized. None foresaw any of this. The tall lad known as Skyscraper on his CB, who is otherwise called Gethin and is still alive and well, but going bald, had a poster on his wall showing a farmer on a tractor, and words by R.S. Thomas arguing the downside of progress:

Ah, but you should see Cynddylan on a tractor...
Riding to work now, as a great man should,
He is the knight at arms breaking the fields'
Mirror of silence, emptying the wood
Of foxes and squirrels and bright jays.

Siop Y Pethe sold many hundreds of that anti-tractor poster over the years. It went out of print only six years ago, which just shows the kind of pull the past exercises. In fact, the same can be said of one of Gethin's other posters, that more famous one of Che Guevara, which still manages to retain its charisma and appears on T-shirts. A strange bedfellow for R.S. Thomas, you might think. Perhaps, but somehow both priest and revolutionary managed to share the same mixed bag of anti-Establishment ideals, which characterized those days, when everyone was allowed a voice, and used it to argue politics. Was it just a naïveté bred by the welfare state that made people think life was about how to live, not about how to survive, and to win?

*Huw Lawrence*

# CHAPTER 3
## House and Family History

*A page from the family Bible.*

## MAM: Mother's Aberystwyth Mariners

I was always sorry that I had not asked my mother more about her side of the family, at a time when she would have been able to tell me, and I wish I'd paid more attention to the stories she would tell me about her holidays on the farm, and Capt. Johnnie Brown's adventures in his seafaring days, 'Around the Horn'. During my research I found that my mother's side of the family,

the Thomases and the Claytons, were nearly all at sea, and several intermarried and lived together while their husbands were at sea. A number of them died at sea. I was always led to believe that my grandfather, who worked in the Post Office, also wanted to go to sea, but that his mother wouldn't let him as he was the youngest and several of his brothers had been lost at sea. This was not actually the case; he was in fact an only child, but his father was one of ten children, nine boys,

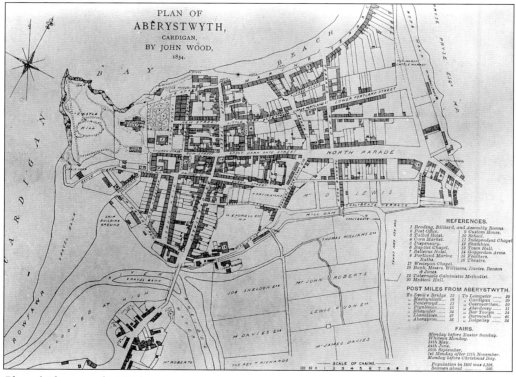

REFERENCES.

1 Reading, Billiard, and Assembly Rooms.
2 Post Office.
3 Talbot Hotel.
4 Corn Market.
5 Dispensary.
6 Baptist Chapel.
7 Bellevue Hotel.
8 Portland Marine Baths.
9 Custom House.
10 School.
11 Independent Chapel
12 Shambles.
13 Town Hall.
14 Goggerdan Arms.
15 Feathers.
16 Theatre.

17 Wesleyan Chapel.
18 Bank, Messrs. Williams, Davies, Benson & Jones.
19 Tabernacle Calvinistic Methodist.
20 Medical Hall.

POST MILES FROM ABERYSTWYTH.

To Devil's Bridge ... 12 | To Lampeter ...... 19
  „ Machynlleth.... 18 | „ Cardigan ........ 39
  „ Ponterwyd..... 11 | „ Caermarthen.. 60
  „ Pisgllimm...... 15 | „ Aberdovey ...... 11
  „ Rhayader...... 34 | „ Dar Towyn ... 14
  „ Llanidloes..... 27 | „ Barmouth ...... 46
  „ Aberayron.... 16 | „ Dolgelley ...... 34

FAIRS.

Monday before Easter Sunday.
Whitsun Monday.
14th May.
24th June.
16th September.
1st Monday after 11th November.
Monday before Christmas Day.

Population in 1831 was 4,128.
Seamen about ...... 500.

Plan of Aberystwyth, 1834.

who had all gone to sea, and several of those were the ones who had not returned.

The other branch of my mother's side was Hopkins, who were farmers in the parishes of Llanbadarn and Llanfihangel y Creuddyn, quite a contrast.

Another contrast was my father's side, the Hamers and the Hughes. Both sides lived in Llanidloes, were as close as the Thomases and Claytons, but were all employed in the nineteenth century woollen industry.

I have selected a few characters to introduce to you from my mother's family, starting with the Claytons, but will look at those in the early part of the nineteenth century only.

In 1841 there were 140 Thomases out of a town population of 4,916, while in 1951 there were 158 out of 5,191, and in *Footprints in the Sand of Time*, reference is made on p. 54 to the Claytons: 'Another name woven into the fabric of Aberystwyth's social history is that of Clayton'. Over many years, members of the Clayton family ' followed the sea', and one such was Isaac Clayton who in 1851 was listed as a master mariner. He lived in Shipbuilders' Row. Each of the four censuses lists numerous Claytons.

But first, a look at Aberystwyth during the early part of the nineteenth century. The map shows the town at that time based around the harbour, although many current features are to be seen. According to Pigot's Directory of 1835, p. 733, Aberystwyth was 'a seaport town, and one of the most fashionable watering places in Wales.' It had been for several years improving its appearance with elegant houses and handsome public buildings. Improvements planned at that time included lighting the town with gas and adding a new harbour, the construction of which was imminent, to include the establishment of a steam packet service. When these improvements had been completed it was believed that Aberystwyth would become 'a great commercial port'. Already it had an extensive trade and commerce industry, exporting lead and silver ore from the mines in the north west of the county; calamine, black leads, wheat and other grains; oak bark and timber; and slate. At the same time it imported porter, wine and other liquors, groceries, salt, coals and linen cloths. Coaches would run regular services to Barmouth, Cheltenham (to link with London), Hereford, Kidderminster, Shrewsbury and Worcester, while regular passenger shipping services would call at Bristol, Liverpool and London.

## The Clayton Family

John Clayton, Master Mariner, was born on 15 August 1815. He married Mary (1826-1897), and they lived at Railway Terrace. They had six children, including Mary and another girl who became Mrs Davies. He captained the *Janet Elizabeth* and the *Mary Jane*, a 39-ton schooner built in Aberystwyth for coasting in 1845/47. It had one deck, two masts, was 14ft 6in long and 14ft 2in across, with planning bowsprit and square stern. John owned all sixty-four shares but on 28 April 1847 he transferred them by Bill of Sale as a mortgage to Anne Watkins, widow, who, on 3 March 1857, returned them to John. He was also Master of the *John James*, a 78-ton schooner built in Aberystwyth between 1859 and 1879. In the Crew Agreement, dated 6 July 1875, preparation was made for the journey from Portmadoc to Reykjavik, Iceland, and thence to any ports in Norway or Lapland, and if required, to any

*The* Credo.

other port on the continent of Europe, and finally to the port of discharge in the United Kingdom, period of engagement not to exceed seven months. The crew of four, Humphrey Williams, bosun, and able seamen Robert Smith, Edward Humphreys (who signed by way of a mark), and John's son, Richard, also agreed to work at all cargoes and ballast as may be required. On 1 May 1861 John captained the *John James* from Llanelli to San Sebastian and back to Liverpool. During the voyage the crew had 1lb bread each day, pork or beef daily, ¾lb each of flour and peas on alternate days. On three days a week they received ½oz tea, ½oz of coffee and 2oz of sugar, as well as 3 quarts of water daily. He added that the scale of provisions to be allowed and served to the crew, in addition to the daily issue of lime, lemon juice and sugar, were sufficient of every necessary food and no waste. He gave all four members of this crew 'Very Good' for their general conduct and for their ability in seamanship, and paid them on 18 June 1861.

*Mourning card for Thomas Clayton.*

Richard Clayton was born in 1819. As a Master Mariner, he married Ann Lloyd, daughter of Thomas Lloyd on 13 Febraury 1846 at Llanbadarn Fawr parish church. They then lived at No. 26 High Street with Ann's parents, Thomas (mariner) and Jane Lloyd. When Richard died, Ann married John Evans, draper. In his will, Richard left all his possessions to Ann. They had one daughter, Jane Ellen Clayton. Richard was a seaman on the *Providence, Star and Pilot*, (these three were coasting vessels), *Luck*, *Earl of Lisburne* (built in 1836) and *Credo*. The brig *Credo* was built in Sunderland in 1833, and she was registered and owned in Aberystwyth. She made several trips to America and Canada with emigrants from Wales. She was abandoned in the mid Atlantic in 1872 without loss of life.

Thomas Clayton was born in Aberystwyth on 20 December 1812. He married Ann, born either in Scotland or at Preston. Ann died in 1895 and Thomas on 8 March 1903, at the age of ninety-one. At that time he was the oldest

resident in Aberystwyth. They had seven children: John (Master Mariner), Mary-Ann, Jane, Betsey, Elinor, Elizabeth and Margaret. Most of their children were born in Birkenhead, but later they lived in Prospect Street.

Thomas first went to sea at the age of twelve as a seaman. On 14 August 1864, he captained the *Messenger* on a journey from Cardiff and Llanelli to Montreal and Quebec and back, on a journey not expected to exceed twelve months. He had a crew of nine, including his seventeen-year-old son, John, as an able seaman. For the journey the scale of provisions to be provided included: 1lb bread, $1\frac{1}{2}$lb of beef, $1\frac{1}{2}$lb of pork, $\frac{1}{2}$lb flour, $\frac{1}{3}$lb of peas, $\frac{1}{8}$oz tea, $\frac{1}{2}$oz coffee, 2oz sugar and 3 quarts of water per day. It was noted in the Agreement of the crew, 'No grog allowed'.

Isaac Clayton was born on 29 October 1810 and married Elizabeth Lloyd in Llanbadarn Fawr parish church on 5 February 1836. They had seven daughters and lived at No. 3 in Shipbuilders' Row, Aberystwyth, in 1851, moving next door by 1861, where they stayed. In 1861, seventy-seven-year-old Elizabeth Davies lived with them as a house servant. Isaac began his last voyage in 1886, drowning on 11 January 1886, aged seventy-five.

**The Next Generation**

Richard Clayton was a son of John Clayton and Mary. He was born in 1858, in Birkenhead and became a Master Mariner.

William Clayton, son of William and Elizabeth, was born on 4 February 1842 in Aberystwyth. His wife was a Miss Owens; they lived on Shipbuilders' Row. He was a boy on the Britannia in 1854/55, and became Mate and then Master on a number of ships. He sailed from Liverpool to Bahia on 8 October 1873, dying at Maceio (Brazil) on 9 March 1874.

## The Thomas Family

Evan Thomas, son of Evan and Elizabeth, was born in Borth on 10 March 1805. He married Ann James in Llanbadarn on 10 February 1826. They had ten children, one of whom was my great grandfather James, born 29 June 1841.

John Thomas was born to Evan and Ann on 23 May 1848 and, like many of his family, went to sea. He was a mate on the *Wellington* and *Rheidol Queen*, before becoming a Master Mariner. When on the *Rheidol Queen*, one of his journeys was to St John's, Newfoundland, then on to other ports in the British North American provinces, the United States of America between Portland and Galveston, the west coast of South America, Cape Colony, the West Indies, the Mediterranean Sea and the Baltic, and back to the United Kingdom, for a voyage not exceeding two years.

For this journey, on which Richard Humphreys was a seaman earning £3 10s per month, John was paid £5 5s per month. Throughout the voyage each crew member received 1lb bread, either $\frac{1}{2}$lb beef or $\frac{1}{2}$lb pork, 1oz tea, $\frac{1}{2}$oz coffee, 2oz sugar, 3 quarts of water per day with $\frac{1}{2}$ lb flour and $\frac{1}{3}$ lb peas on alternate days, with the proviso that an equivalent may be issued at the Master's option. No spirits were allowed!

From 1861 to 1867 John also captained the *Volunteer*, a 65-ton schooner, built in Aberystwyth, by James for E. Jones. On 23 September 1861 his ship arrived at Aberystwyth harbour with a general cargo from Liverpool; on 7 September 1862 with a cargo of limestone and slate from Port Dinorwic. On one occasion in 1874 both *Hope* and *Wellington* left Darien in the Panama isthmus at the same time, with a cargo of pitch pine, and raced each other back to Aberystwyth. The *Wellington* won, taking less than the forty-seven days it took the Hope to reach Aberystwyth

harbour, where the crew were paid off. For the journey, the mate received £5 5s per month, the bosun and the cook were each paid £4 10s, and the ship's boy £2. The provision allowed on board per man per week for this journey were 7lb bread; 6lb beef; $3\frac{1}{2}$lb pork; $1\frac{1}{2}$lb flour; 1 pint peas; 5lb rice; $\frac{7}{8}$oz leaf tea; $3\frac{1}{2}$oz coffee; 14oz sugar; 6 pints water per day for washing, cooking and drinking!

At the start of the twentieth century, the Aberystwyth photographer, H.H. Davies, took the photograph (see p. 56) of three generations of the Thomas family. Standing at the back is James, with a full beard and moustache, and his son, Isaac Clayton, sporting a neat moustache and short, parted hair. Both men are fairly formally dressed in what were probably their best woollen cloth suits; Isaac has a hard collar. At the front on the left is Mary Jane, wife of Isaac. She would then have been about thirty years old. Both she and James's wife, Jane Ellen, on the other side of the seat, are wearing what are probably one-piece sedate, dark dresses. According to costume analyst Jane Shrimpton, skirts would have been fairly full and reaching almost to the ground; the bodice fits closely to the figure, the shaping achieved with darts at the bust. The most distinguishing feature of women's dresses during this period is the puffed sleeves, often referred to as 'gigot' or 'leg of mutton' sleeves. They were made with a gathered puff at the shoulder, a very full puff on the upper arm, but fitted tightly on the lower arm from elbow to wrist. Jane also appears to be wearing a cape, while both ladies wear jewellery: Mary a simple cross on chain, and possibly a small brooch at the neck and Jane, long beads. Jane's hair was worn centrally parted and drawn

*James Thomas with his family. James is standing at the back with his son, Isaac Clayton Thomas. Mary Jane Thomas with their two children, Ena Clayton and Margaret Jane, and James' wife Jane Ellen (née Clayton) are at the front.*

back into a bun, while Mary's is softer and feminine, of a more loose style, with her bun 'the soft knot' worn higher on her head, with the front hair swept up and puffed over pads, known as 'rats', to achieve the full look. Between Mary and Jane are Mary's two girls: Ena wears a typical style of white cotton baby dress, quite elaborately made with a frilled collar, puffed elbow-length sleeves and flounced hem. Margaret Jane wears a little smock dress, reaching to a few inches below the knee. There is a pretty frill at the shoulders and at the cuffs of the long sleeves. Margaret's hair has by now grown long enough to be in ringlets, while both girls have ribbons in their hair for their occasion of the year.

Isaac Clayton Thomas was born in 1867 to John Thomas and Elizabeth. He married Elizabeth Lloyd and they had two children. He captained the *Cambrian Belle*

from 1879 to 1881. The following article appeared in the Caernarfon and Denbighshire Herald of 16 February 1856:

On Wednesday morning last between eight and nine, a first-rate brig, of 300 tons burthen, was launched from the building yard of Messrs John Evans and Son, the property of Capt Richard Delahoyd, of this town, intended for Mediterranean trade. The vessel is a clipper built in the Aberdeen style, and is allowed to be one of the fastest vessels ever built in this town, and no doubt she will be one of the fastest sailing vessels afloat. This fine brig was named the *Cambrian Belle*. Miss Powell, of Nanteos, surrounded by a great number of ladies and good men, named her in the usual way. A bottle of old port wine was smashed on the occasion. She had to glide upwards of 200 yards from the stocks before reaching her element, which was done majestically, although she was fully rigged. We have had occasion to record launches often, but as on this occasion never was such enthusiasm manifested by the inhabitants, who, although so early, were on Rofawr by thousands. She had the flags of England, France, Turkey, and Sardinia waving above; that of Russia contemptuously below. The building of this splendid vessel does great credit to Mr John Evans, who spent some time, a few years ago, at Aberdeen, and the vessel was built after his drawing, and under his immediate direction. The harbour presented an imposing sight. There were about 130 vessels all with their colours hoisted amidst the roaring cannons and the hurrahs of the multitude.

Soon after the launching, and before the maiden voyage, the Revd John Hughes, the much-respected vicar of Aberystwyth, held a church service on the *Cambrian Belle.*

In this article I have tried to give an outline of life at sea during the first part of the nineteenth century through the records of a few members of my family. Space prevents me continuing!

For copies of the documents that I have used in this article I am very grateful to Ceredigion Museum, the National Library of Wales, the National Maritime Museum and Cardiganshire County Library.

*Joy Hamer*

## A House and its Residents: a Story of Borth Mariners

David Jones, mariner, who married Anne Hughes at Llanfihangel Genau'r Glyn parish church on 8 February 1861, built Seaview House in the same year. David

*Ena and Margaret Jane Thomas in their sailor outfits.*

was twenty-four, his wife twenty-five; Anne is listed in the census of 1861 as living at Morfa Borth and is described simply as 'wife'. Ten years later, at the census of 1871, she is described as 'Mariner's wife' aged thirty-five and with three sons: David Hughes aged eight, Edward Jones who was six, and the youngest, John, aged three.

It would seem that the father was always away at sea at census time for he never appears by name in the ten-yearly records, but by 1881 Anne Jones appears as 'Master Mariner's wife' aged forty-five. Two further sons were born during that decade, Morgan H. Jones, then aged nine and Hugh Jones who was five, both being described as 'scholar'. The 1891 census however is the last appearance of Mrs Jones and, by implication, of her husband, as she is by then a 'Master Mariner's widow'. She died in 1899 aged about sixty-three. She had produced five sons, all of them mariners; their master mariner father died in 1891 at Briton Ferry of exhaustion aged only fifty-four. Tragedy had already struck

*Seaview House, 1911.*

the family as young John, the third son, died at sea, washed overboard in 1883 at the age of sixteen.

Seaview House became the property of the eldest son, David, on his mother's death, who was himself by then a master mariner. In 1920 David Hughes Jones, master mariner, of South Pacific, Barry Dock and No. 8 Cambrian Terrace, Borth, sold Seaview House which was subsequently more than doubled in size, renamed Maesarfor and, in 1968, became the property of the author of this article. We had been led into the history of the Jones family by tracing the development of our house back to its beginnings. The photograph (above) was taken around 1911 and shows David Hughes Jones and his family in front of Seaview House with its central front door. The front door is now on the north side, but it is possible to see from the outline in the ceiling of one of the downstairs rooms, where the walls had been, including a passage to the front door. The

many changes made in 1920 were to ensure that the house was secure against the sea as well as to enlarge it.

The Jones family, however, spread into other houses in Borth. Apart from the eldest son in Cambrian Terrace, who died in 1935, Edward Jones, the second son, owned Glanmor and died in 1925; Captain Morgan H. Jones, the fourth son, lived at Glendower and died aged forty-eight in 1920; and in 1906 Capt. Hugh Jones bought Surrey House, next door to Seaview, which subsequently became the Surrey Café and is currently The Bay fish and chip shop. The house still bears the name Surrey, which was named after a ship.

Hugh Jones, the youngest of the five boys, continued the tragic destiny of the family. In October 1918, less than a month before the end of the First World War, his ship SS *Heath Park* was torpedoed off Bilbao in the Bay of Biscay. He and his nephew, David Kenneth Jones, the son of Edward of Glanmor, both died, as did another Borth mariner, David Llywelyn Lewis of Dalston House. I have

*Capt. Hugh Jones.*

*Capt. Hugh Jones with his crew 1910-1918.*

*Von Glasenapp, 2 January 1917.*

blacked out steamer on easterly course with torpedo fire. To establish the identity of the steamer, a piece of wreck was taken onboard. After this engagement it was the armed English steamer, Heath Park, 1963t, with 3500t iron ore from Bilbao to Maryport, Solway Forth [sic]. Soon after, another steamer of the same size about 2000t on an easterly course, through torpedo fire. Ship sunk at once. Name could not be established. Also later evidence failed to ascertain the identity of the ship.

That was Capt. von Glasenapp's bag for one day's hunting in the Atlantic, leaving numerous widows and orphans in a trail of indiscriminate murder on the high seas; several of the victims were aboard ships of neutral countries.

This tale of a Borth family is, I think, representative. All the rigours and dangers of life at sea can be traced in this one family's history. Even when they were not drowned at sea most of them died relatively young. Their story can be traced in the cemetery in Llandre where there is a memorial to David Jones (1836-1891), 'bu farw yn Briton Ferry', and of his son John (1867-1883), and another to Edward Jones of Glanmor, Borth, which carries the inscription: 'Also of their youngest son David Kenneth born 19th October 1901, lost at sea by his ship, SS *Heath Park*, being torpedoed by the enemy off the Spanish coast 5th October 1918.' The Lewis family gravestone also records the death of David Llywelyn, lost at sea with SS *Heath Park*.

The war memorial on the cliff top in Borth appropriately looks out to sea. The largest proportion of names recorded is from the Merchant Navy. It was said that it was a common sight in Aberystwyth to see the Borth widows coming over the hill to sell seafood gathered from the rocks under the cliff. The sea-faring people of Borth also have their memorial in the writings of the late A.

learned of the fate of Hugh Jones from his daughter, Mrs Kathleen Evans, who was only one year old when her father was killed. Her late husband Ron Evans lent me a copy, in German, of the log of the U-boat that sunk the Heath Park and many other ships on its lethal voyage between 15 September and 26 October 1918. U 91 under the command of Capt. von Glasenapp sailed from Heligoland around the Hebrides, down the west coast of France and back through the Pentland Firth to Germany. The log records the sinking of twelve vessels from Denmark, France, Spain, Portugal, Norway, and the British Heath Park. The log entry for 5 October reads as follows (my translation):

In morning in darkness, in front of the southern part of the French west coast, a single

*Seaview House, 2001.*

Edward Richards, whose short stories and radio plays gave literary expression of some distinction to the tragic and sometimes comic lives of his local characters. I wrote an article* about his work in the *New Welsh Review* after having traced his short stories in various journals in the National Library of Wales and being given, by his widow, the typescripts of his two radio plays, *Who'll Buy my Fresh Herrings*, broadcast in 1951, and *Master Mariner*, broadcast in 1956 and 1960. The typescripts have been deposited in the National Library and were given a public reading in Borth in 1978, a year before Ted Richards died. They illustrate dramatically the story, which I have attempted to extract from the census and churchyard records of the Jones family of Seaview House, Borth.

* Matthews, David A. 'A. Edwards Richards: writer from Mid Wales', *New Welsh Review* 26, autumn 1994, pp. 46-50. The article is followed by the first publication of a story by Richards called 'The Spanish Lady'.

*David Matthews*

## Aberystwyth Disasters

The magnificent memorial erected on the castle grounds records a sad reminder of the wars. It is one of the finest to be built. After the First World War, warships made annual visits to the bay with townspeople being allowed on board.

On 20 February 1935, a terrific fire was witnessed in the centre of town. The building was the Palladium, which housed Peacock's stores on the ground floor, with a picture-house above, and stood on the corner of Eastgate and Market Street. The area stood empty for many years afterwards, but now has been built upon.

Fierce storms hit the locality during 1938, with much damage being done. During this storm so much damage was done to Victoria Terrace that all the women students in Alexandra Hall were sent home. The damage was done by debris that was hurled with such terrific force by the waves, that the area looked like a bomb site. When clearing the area, some of the stones and flagstones took three men to lift. Basements were flooded, and many had to be rescued from their beds. Roll calls were

*The interior of Peacocks after the fire, 1935.*

*Hafod church fire, 1932.*

*Waterloo Hotel fire damage, August 1919.*

*Storm damage to the pier, 1938.*

made at the many hotels that were on the promenade to make sure all had been rescued. The Pier cinema carried on showing films, although the end of the pier had been cut off.

After clearing up the rubble, it was decided that some improvements had to be made to prevent a recurrence. A cofferdam was constructed but was itself badly damaged in a further storm on 23 November 1938.

My grandmother kept a boarding house in Castle Terrace. My grandparents contracted smallpox in 1903, having been infected by a visitor from Birmingham. They were then sent to Tan y Bwlch isolation hospital. This was not the one used as a hospital at a later date, but a small cottage on the beach, in a true sense a cottage hospital. There was a nurse and handyman here. My grandparents were in isolation for some time; my grandmother was pregnant at the time and a daughter was born to her on 23 April 1904, with no ill effects. She was referred to as the 'smallpox baby'. While in isolation at the hospital, my grandparents wanted some personal shopping. Jenkin Humphreys (latterly an auctioneer in the town) was the messenger for the hospital. He would deliver goods as far as the bridge over the Ystwyth, which was on the route to the hospital, and the nurse would then collect them. Everyone dreaded catching smallpox. There was one incident when my grandmother sent money to the messenger to buy a comb. When the shopkeeper heard whom the comb was for, he sent the comb but refused the money in case it was infected.

This cottage was a very poor isolation hospital and this was reported to Parliament during this time. This resulted in the new hospital being built in Pen yr Angor, and the old hospital remained unoccupied for many years. The cottage then became a home for the Linett family. On 15 January 1938, early in the morning during a storm, the cottage was razed to the ground with elderly Mrs Linett and her two daughters inside. The family had battled against the elements all night, but a

*Building the cofferdam, 1938.*

*The Palladium on fire, 1935.*

*Victoria Terrace after the storm of 15 January 1938.*

tremendous wave defeated them. The railway line ran nearby and a light engine was going by. The driver and the fireman heard screams coming from the direction of the beach. They reported what they had seen when they reached Llanilar station, thus alerting the police to the family's plight. It is a coincidence that the fireman, Tom Millichip, was the husband of the 'smallpox baby'. Both the Linett daughters had been buried up to their necks in rubble and twenty workmen were dispatched with picks and axes. The daughters were conscious, and inquired about their mother. A further search was made and Mrs Linett was found clinging to a table, having been washed from the cottage down to the riverbank. They suffered shock and exposure and Mrs Linett had a broken leg.

*Delyth M. Jones*

## Aberystwyth Transport

My grandfather, Thomas Morgan, was born at Bryngwyn Farm and brought up in Nantyrhydd, both in Capel Seion. During his earlier days he was a champion ploughman, winning trophies in almost all the ploughing matches held, from Capel Seion to Cemmaes Road. When he gave up ploughing, he was much in demand as a judge in such contests. He moved to Aberystwyth in 1896 and became foreman in Messrs Jones brothers, North Parade. Aberystwyth, at that time, was a thriving holiday resort with an influx of visitors from the Midlands and, during the Miners' Fortnight, from South Wales. The firm where he worked specialized in conveying people, especially visitors, on drives to various locations. Horse-drawn vehicles conveyed them in the days before motorization.

Another of his duties was to take the Judge from his lodgings in Lampeter to the Lampeter Assizes, in a landau drawn by two horses. One was Judge Avery and another Judge Jelf. To carry out this duty, he had to shave off his moustache and wear a uniform. The uniform consisted of a huntsman-green face-cloth coat with gold buttons and mustard colour facings on the collar and sleeves; white doe-skin breeches with black riding boots; and a silk hat with a cockade ribbon on it. This was a very important occasion for him. The cab had to be spick and span, and the horses' coats and harnesses had to be gleaming. During this time, my grandfather would stay in Lampeter.

Horses were used to pull the lifeboat to the promenade to set out to sea and for exhibitions. This always drew crowds of sightseers. The inhabitants of Aberystwyth benefited greatly from these visitors, and different venues provided plenty of entertainment.

After working for this firm for a few years, he was sent to London to learn how to drive a motor car. The art of driving a car in those days was much more complicated than it is today, but one did not encounter many other vehicles on the roads, which were quite rough at that time. He soon mastered the controls of motor vehicles. During the first decade of the twentieth century, he was again sent to London, this time to fetch a charabanc, and it was claimed that it was he who had the honour of driving the first charabanc into Wales. A driver had to accompany him and stay in Aberystwyth, to teach him how to drive this new vehicle. The journey from London was quite tedious and took two days to complete as he was limited to 12 miles per hour. Later his son, Tommy, joined the staff of Jones Brothers and such was his attraction to the motor car, that he went over to America in 1919 to work in the Ford Motor Works in Detroit and stayed there for a few years.

*Thomas Morgan setting out to fetch the judge.*

*Thomas Morgan holding the reins outside the Falcon Hotel, Llanilar 1906.*

*Thomas Morgan in charge of the horses drawing the lifeboat on the promenade, 1906.*

*Thomas Morgan in the driving seat during Coronation celebrations outside the railway station, 1911.*

*Father and son, Thomas and Tommy Morgan in the driving seats outside Royal Oak Llanfarian.*

*Thomas Morgan in the driving seat outside the Hafod Arms Hotel.*

*Thomas Morgan on the road between Newquay and Llandysul.*

*Tommy Morgan and passengers take a break in Aberffrwd, 1914.*

These vehicles, whether horse-drawn or motorized, were given names: Countess, Blodwen, Cymro and Sais. The ladies wore motoring veils to hold their hats securely while travelling. Marketing was quite important in those days, with charabanc excursions being advertised to various locations. The boards advertise excursions to places quite far from Aberystwyth. Evening excursions cost 3s.

*Delyth M. Jones*

## Cwmystwyth School, 1904-1960

It is, I suppose, not everyone's choice to live in a converted school, but it has some advantages. One of them is that if one is interested in the history of where one lives, there is an official record of just that in the contents of the log that the head teacher was required to maintain. Much of that log is of the mundane and routine nature of school life, but there are many entries which are interesting, even amusing, which throw an intriguing light on school-life in the years before, between and after the two World Wars.

Cwmystwyth School was built in 1903/04 on land leased by T.J. Waddingham of Hafod to Llanfihangel-y-Creuddyn Upper United District School Board for a ground rent of £2 2s per annum. The lease is signed by T.J. Waddingham and witnessed by George Cook, 'Butler at Hafod'. In May 1904 the building was completed and passed for use and we have the first entries in the log:

6 Jun 04 At 3 p.m. all the children marched from the old school to the new school, carrying as much apparatus as they could. (No doubt the operation was carried out with military precision.)

7 Jun 04 The pupils commenced working in the new school. The attendance was 75.

However, it was not long before trouble was brewing.

16 Jun 04 Corporal punishment had to be administered on Thomas Oliver for killing a gosling.

Just what the punishment was is not recorded. This is one of only two entries in the log regarding corporal punishment. Knowing the general practice in schools of the period, one wonders whether the pupils were remarkably well behaved or whether such occasions were too frequent to merit recording.

Anyway, by 1923 tactics had changed:

12 Jun 23 Martha Jones was of such continuous bad behaviour that she had to be sent home until her mother could improve her behaviour.

Much attention is given in the log to attendance, for example:

October 1907 Only 26 children out of 73 were present due to the Whooping Cough epidemic.

References to such epidemics appear almost every year. Nevertheless, attendance was apparently better than other schools in the area since:

6 Oct 08 The Attendance Officer brought the flag to school for best attendance in the area over the quarter.

This flag passed from school to school according to which could show the best attendance records. Several entries appear in the Log regarding the award of the flag over the years. All sorts of excuses for low attendance are given: illness, snow, floods, shearing, haymaking, fair days, having to walk 3 miles to school, etc. Things seem to have come to a head when, in May 1911, one Annie James took over as temporary head teacher. She records:

30 Jun 11 Attendance low because of shearing. It is custom here, which should be put down by the LEA, for all children to attend

shearing at certain farms, where they can be of no earthly use but to get in the way. The Attendance Officer purposely absents himself from the school on these occasions.

26 Jul 11 Attendance low again because of haymaking. Everything seems to be allowed to interfere with the attendance at this school.

26 Sept 11 Attendance low again. The children are too fatigued to come to school after yesterday's fair.

However, she did not last long and was replaced that November; nor did her outbursts seem to have had any effect, for right through to 1941 we find entries such as 'School closed for the potato harvest' and 'School closed annually for shearing and for the Aberystwyth Hiring Fair'.

Another major factor interfering with schoolwork was the weather, and entries commenting on it abound. For example:

3 Mar 09 Only 8 out of 75 at school because of snow.

19 Sept 22 Worst floods for 35 years. Many children could not get to school.

11 Feb 29 15ft snowdrifts along the road. Children could not get to school.

Jan 1947 Bad snowdrifts up to 10 ft... impossible to open the school door... drifts above the school gates... no fresh meat for a month... bread, oil, and the bare essentials sent by train to Crosswood, then lorry to Pontrhydygroes, where men of the village collected goods in sacks and carried them home 3 to 7 miles on foot.

10 Feb 47 Six ex-sevicemen volunteered to go over the hill to Devil's Bridge to fetch a coffin sent up from Aberystwyth and to carry it back to the village. The whole village is a bare vastness of snow. There are no roads, bushes or trees visible. Hundreds of sheep have perished and carcasses abound everywhere.

Throughout the whole time the heating of the classrooms and the chimneys seem to have been a problem. The following is a selection of many entries:

Mar 1916 School closed because of no coal.

10 Feb 19 6 degrees of frost and no fires because of the chimneys.

Jan 1924 It was so cold in the classroom that the ink was frozen in the inkwells, so no written work could be done.

At the other end of the scale, ventilation seems to have been a problem also:

22 Jul 10 The schoolrooms are very hot in the summer. The windows should be made to open.

14 Jul 11 School was dismissed this afternoon because the classrooms were too hot to stay in them and I feared for the health of both the teachers and the children.

School life was not quite devoid of the odd bit of excitement:

23 Jul 12 A regiment of soldiers passed through the village today. The children were marched into the playground to see them.... [Later] A 'sham fight' in the village between the Northumberland Fusiliers and the Yorks and Staffs Regiment. Children were marched up Y Glog and an open-air lesson on the battle was given by the Headmaster.

Another noteworthy event of a different kind was the visit of the dentist to the school. There is nothing unusual in that, but the record of the event was quaint to say the least:

14 Feb 42 Mr Byron Lloyd, the dentist, visited the school today and extracted the children's teeth. What – all of them?

The comments of the HMI on the state of the building after his periodic visits were forthright: 'Premises in a very bad state of repair... Interior walls and window frames rotting... Kitchen range out of action ... The 'offices' [a choice piece of euphemism!] are of the old pail type and in a dilapidated condition.' The last comment was made in 1946, but seems to have had little effect, as in

1952 we read that 'no water is connected to the 'offices' which are still of the old pail type.'

There was great excitement in November 1951:

27 Nov 51 Fire in the school kitchen. At 8 p.m. Dai Roberts of Gate Cottage saw lights under the slates and informed the Head Teacher who went to investigate. Slates were being blown off and a portion of the roof was a mass of flames… We entered the kitchen and saw flames emerging into the room from above the chimney pipe of the cooking range. Mr Roberts went for Mr Evans of Penybont, who phoned the Fire Brigade. I called on two neighbours from The Lodge to help. Buckets of water and a stirrup pump were organised. Then Messrs Alun and Gwyn arrived. All with the aid of other villagers were getting the fire under control when the Fire Brigade arrived.

The school survived, but what the fire could not do, depopulation of the village did, and with only five pupils left the inevitable happened. The final entries in the log make sad reading.

24 May 60 Meeting of parents, Governors and Directors to consider the Closure Notice received.

1 Jul 60 Three copies of Closure Notice received.

22 Jul 60 Cwmystwyth School closed.

The final entry in the Log reads:

31 Aug 60 The past half-century has been a period of change; today sees Britain as thickly studded with TV masts as the birthday cake of an octogenarian with candles… Along the highways cars rush in a frantic attempt to travel between two points in the shortest possible time. To such a world, the closure of a small village school is a matter of little importance; and yet for some of us it spells the end of a way of life, where the village school has been the centre of the cultural as well as the scholastic life of the community… The inevitable centralisation of community services is tidier and commercially sounder, but what of the gaps left? It is to be hoped that the Welshman will retain his highly individual way of thinking and of life despite bureaucracy and centralisation.

*Mari Evans, Head Teacher*

Acknowledgement is made to The National Library of Wales and to the Ceredigion County Archivist for access to the Cwmystwyth School Head Teachers' Log.

*D.E. Hoare*

# CHAPTER 4

## Town Area and History

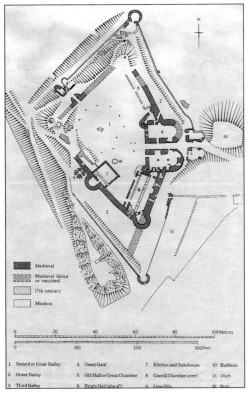

Medieval
Medieval fallen
or vanished
17th century
Modern

| 0 | 20 | 40 | 60 | 80 | 100 Metres |
|---|---|---|---|---|---|
| 0 | 100 | 200 | | 300 Feet | |

1. Second or Inner Bailey
2. Outer Bailey
3. Third Bailey
4. Great Gate
5. Old Hall or Great Chamber
6. King's Hall (site of?)
7. Kitchen and Bakehouse
8. Cnevill Chamber (over)
9. Lime Kiln
10. Barbican
11. Ditch
W. Well

Site map of Aberystwyth Castle

### The Secrets of Aberystwyth Castle

My first visit to Aberystwyth Castle was in
October 1975, shortly after I took up my new
job as an investigator with the Royal
Commission on the Ancient and Historical
Monuments of Wales, which was then based in

Edleston House on Queen's Road. It was to be
the beginning of twenty-six years of study of
the site, which still continues.

In those days the site looked very
different from its present appearance. The
much-reconstructed outer curtain-wall and
its north and south towers were similar to
now, as were the familiar landmarks of the
north-west tower on the north-west line of the
inner curtain, and the northern half of the
Great Gate. Most of the rest of the site,
however, was covered by grass mounds and
terraces and paths laid out at the end of the
eighteenth century. At several points along
these mounds large blocks of castle masonry lay
protruding above the surface. Some earlier
clearance had revealed a stairway, passage and
fireplace in the south wall of the south
chamber of the Great Gate, but this was
otherwise only visible as a tall curving wall
above a grass mound. The site of the castle
well, cleared out many years before, was then
capped with an ugly concrete slab. Modern
features of the site included the Gorsedd circle,
a weather station on the site of the hall at the
south end of the Inner Bailey, and a coastguard
look-out station on the site of the west tower of
the inner curtain-wall.

Local people and visitors alike had little
information available to them to explain the
ruins as they strolled around the castle grounds.
Jack Spurgeon's excellent booklet on the castle
published a few years before gave a good

*Aberystwyth Castle from the tower of St Michael's church, 1976. (Crown Copyright, RCAHMW)*

account of the history of the site derived from medieval and later sources, but was unable to provide much detailed guidance to what was to be seen. The simple reason for this was that nobody really knew, and that without excavation the site and its detailed structural history could not be worked out.

As I walked through the passageway between the chambers of the Great Gate and emerged into the inside yard of the castle (the Inner Bailey), I saw to my right the unmistakable sight of an archaeologist's trench dug along the rear of the middle part of the inner curtain-wall. On returning to my office I soon found out that my colleagues Jack Spurgeon and Eric Whatmore were responsible. They had obtained permission on behalf of the Ceredigion Antiquarian Society to test how much of the wall of the castle might survive under the landscape mounds on the west side, and to lay out the stretch of excavated wall in time for the 700th anniversary celebrations in 1977.

Like most archaeological digs, as soon as spade and trowel were put into the ground the unexpected occurred. The curtain-wall was reasonably well preserved up to a height of 2.3m and had a culvert through it draining into the Outer Bailey. The shape of the mounds over the curtain-wall had suggested the strong possibility of a tower at this point, and the excavators duly uncovered the blocked door to it. What they had not anticipated was finding a narrow stone wall bonded in brown clay running parallel, 1.5m inside the inner curtain, at the north-west end of which was the base of an oven. Other interesting features found in the narrow passage formed at the back of the tower by the narrow wall and the oven were two low stone and clay benches. A medieval record refers to a stable and bakehouse under one roof below the wall on the west side, built in 1286, and it was understandable that the excavators should think that they had found them. However, there were already clues in some of the finds, such as pottery and window glass, that there were significant later occupations in parts of the site, especially in the first half of the seventeenth century. Later work would show that although the

*Aberystwyth Castle: the interior of the Great Gate before excavation. (Crown Copyright, RCAHMW)*

*Aberystwyth Castle: the north-west tower from the third bailey, before excavation. (Crown Copyright, RCAHMW)*

*Aberystwyth Castle: the Inner Bailey and north-west tower before the excavations. (Crown Copyright, RCAHMW)*

*Aerystwyth Castle: The south-east outer curtain-wall and south tower before excavations. The garden occupies the site of a rock-cut ditch. (Crown Copyright, RCAHMW)*

*Aberystwyth Castle, 1975 excavation. Early in the excavation the diggers revealed the north-west inner curtain wall beneath the landscaper's rubble. (Crown Copyright, RCAHMW)*

interpretation of the buildings as a stable and bread oven was correct, the benches probably acting as bases for mangers or troughs, they dated to the seventeenth rather than the late thirteenth century.

The dig of summer 1975 achieved its purpose but also threw up some interesting problems about whether to and how to proceed with further digging. By the end of the year I had become fully involved in the project, and Peter Smith, the Secretary of the Royal Commission, allowed Jack and myself to act as general directors of a much more ambitious project to excavate a long expanse of the south-west Outer Bailey. I had convinced my colleagues that the problems of the castle could not be solved by small-scale trenching, but by larger area excavation. To do this was beyond the means of the local society, but by good fortune 1976 saw the start of the large schemes

for unemployed persons directed by the Manpower Services Commission. Jack and myself approached the owners of the site, Ceredigion District Council as it was then called and, through the good offices of the Director of Technical Services, W. Price-Jones, and his staff, we were able to persuade the Council to sponsor an MSC scheme. This was to be the pattern for the coming years until 1988. A site supervisor who had archaeological experience was appointed to the day-to-day management of the excavations, directing a team of unemployed people, whilst the strategic and academic oversight of the work was the responsibility of Jack and me. I cannot praise too highly the efforts made by Ceredigion Council and its officers to make the excavations and the subsequent renovations a success. The schemes were not only a great success archaeologically,

*Aberystwyth Castle, 1977. The central tower of the north-west inner curtain wall under excavation. The roughly-built bench was constructed in the seventeenth century. (Crown Copyright, RCAHMW)*

*Aberystwyth Castle, 1976-77 excavations. Inside the north-west inner curtain wall are the remains of the seventeenth-century stables and oven. (Crown Copyright, RCAHMW)*

they also provided the basis for permanent, 'real', employment for many of the MSC participants.

The 1976 and 1977 excavations in the south-west Outer Bailey yielded a lot of information about various phases of the castle's history. In the first part of the dig a great deal of attention was paid to understanding the extensive banks of landscaping rubble covering most of the site. They were photographed in detail along with their associated features such as gravel paths and stone bases for benches. A curious feature, and one which was later found in several parts of the site, was the use of beach cobbles at the base of the banks as a sort of foundation course. I am still unsure of the reasons for this practice, but I hope that

research on eighteenth-century landscape gardening practice will provide the answer. The time spent in dissecting these rubble banks was worth it, because in later digs we had a much better appreciation of them and of how they differed from other rubble deposits on the site, allowing us to deal with them more efficiently. The very large lumps of masonry that stood in the bank on the site of the central tower of the inner curtain were originally thought to have been in the positions they had fallen to after the slighting of the castle in 1649 by Parliamentary troops. Our excavations proved that this was not the case here nor, later, elsewhere. The blocks had been levered into position on top of the banks by the late eighteenth-century landscapers to indicate the sub-surface position of significant structures such as towers, which they must have partially uncovered during their work.

After several months of the very hot summer of 1976 a JCB was brought in to clear the landscape rubbles. Immediately it revealed the outer face of the inner curtain, which ran in a series of slightly angled facets, and the rounded front of the central tower. Neither was very well preserved, but both contained enough features to add considerably to our previous knowledge of the site. The other opening of the culvert through the curtain-wall south of the tower was revealed, and from it there stretched a crudely-dug ditch across the ward. This ditch was full of bone refuse, mainly of cattle, representing on-site butchery in the first half of the seventeenth century. In the middle of the ward was a crude hearth of unknown date.

As we cleared to the north of the tower the first important clue to the complicated early history of the castle emerged. Patches of burnt earth were excavated and groups of burnt stones were noticed in the face of the adjacent curtain-wall. Soon the unmistakable outline of a limekiln with a single chamber served by four flues emerged, and subsequent excavation showed that it had been fired by coal. Its proximity and relationship to the inner curtain-wall made it clear that the kiln had been built before the wall was started. This was the first indication that the outer and inner curtains were begun at slightly different dates, and that the concentric plan of the castle that is

*Aberystwyth Castle, 1983. The hall in the south angle of the inner bailey. The large wall down the middle of the hall may have formed part of the seventeenth-century mint. (Crown Copyright, RCAHMW)*

so familiar to us may not have been part of the original design. In all our excavations we have only found one limekiln, which was surely inadequate for the needs of the site. The medieval records suggest an shortage of appropriate building materials in several areas, and a dramatic illustration of this is our discovery that much of the lower part of the thick inner curtain-wall was built largely of rubble and clay with only a small amount of lime mortar for the facing. It was only bonded throughout with lime mortar in its upper sections.

Besides giving new insights into the early phases of the castle these excavations also gave important information about the end of the site as an effective fortification. In casual conversation the castle is spoken of as having been blown up by Cromwell's troops. It was certainly largely demolished in 1649, but the process was probably mining. Having cleared the front face of the tower wall we found a hollow containing an upright charred beam of oak. The simplest explanation for this feature was that a hole had been gouged in the face of the wall, not a difficult task given its poor construction, and a prop inserted that was fired to help collapse the wall above. A procedure like this carried out around the lower walls would have brought them tumbling down in a fairly controlled way.

The latter stages of this season of digging concentrated on the interior of the tower and finishing off earlier work inside the inner curtain. The main findings in the tower were that it had a polygonal plan originally and that in the seventeenth century it was crudely refitted with a slabbed floor and a firing bench around its sides. Lead shot found in occupation deposits attest to the presence of a military garrison. The construction of the benches and the relationship of deposits in the tower to the oven, benches and narrow wall inside the curtain allowed us to identify the latter also as seventeenth-century structures.

During these excavations we also took the opportunity to clear the south-west outer tower of the north-west gate. It was through this gate that, in medieval times, access was gained to the third bailey of the castle, which occupied the headland where the war memorial now stands. We know from contemporary records that this area was in a state of poor repair as early as the first half of the fourteenth century, suffering from battering by the sea. A ditch separated the main castle from the third bailey, crossed by a wooden bridge from the north-west gate. The bottom of the abutments of the medieval bridge are still visible in the side of the ditch. In 1976, behind an iron gate, you could see a set of crude steps leading up from the ditch between the bases of the two outer towers of the north-west gate. It was probably these that had given rise to the idea that there was some kind of tunnel from the castle into the town. Our dig cleared up this question once and for all. At the back of the tower we found a series of small steps leading down from the floor to the wider steps between the towers. This confirmed our interpretation of the steps as part of a sally port, a means whereby a detachment of troops could launch a surprise attack on a besieging army.

In 1978 and 1979 the MSC scheme concentrated on making a detailed catalogue of the finds from the earlier digs and consolidating the walls of the buildings they had exposed. There is little point in excavating ancient remains if they are not conserved to a high standard and the results of the investigations published fully. Indeed, digging without consolidation and publication is little more than vandalism! Interim accounts of the findings have been published regularly in journals and a full description in book form will be available in a few years' time.

Excavation did not resume until July 1982. The area chosen was in the south angle of the Inner Bailey to the north-east of the earlier dig. The mounds and hollows here had long been thought to be on the site of a hall. At their north end, projecting above ground level, was a straight length of wall at right-angles to the main curtain and blocking off a window in the stair turret of the south chamber of the Great Gate. This wall not only suggested the presence of a large building in the area, but also of one that had been built after the Great Gate, though still in medieval times.

The excavations, supervised by James Thorburn, lasted well into 1983 and added considerably to our knowledge. A large medieval hall was exposed, which, as we suspected, was built after the Great Gate, involving the demolition of an original triangular compartment like that at the rear of the northern chamber of the Great Gate. The east side of the hall was formed by the inner curtain wall in which there was inserted a fireplace with flanking splayed windows. Little remained of the main north-west wall of the hall except a short stub at its south end and the base of a moulded sandstone door jamb. In front of this there had been a narrow corridor, of which only the base of the outer wall survived. This wall may have supported an arcade or row of small columns.

We were unable to tell how long the hall was in use, but by the beginning of the seventeenth century it was probably no more than a shell of broken-down walls. At

Aberystwyth Castle, 1985. The south tower of the north-west inner curtain wall under excavation. The bench is of seventeenth-century origin. (Crown Copyright, RCAHMW)

Aberystwyth Castle, 1984. Arched latrine outlets near the south tower of the north-west inner curtain wall. (Crown Copyright, RCAHMW)

this time a stone and clay wall, 1.2m wide, was built down the length of the main chamber of the hall. Its construction resembled closely that of the wall found inside the inner curtain in the 1975 dig

Associated with the wall in the hall were some very interesting features. The original windows of the medieval hall in the inner curtain-wall were blocked and converted into alcoves. A small rectangular room or enclosure was created at the north-east end of the new wall by building a short length of clay and stone wall at right-angles to the north-east end wall of the medieval hall. James Thorburn found evidence in the destruction debris on the site that the seventeenth-century building was probably half-timbered and roofed with slates.

We know that Thomas Bushell established a royal mint in the castle in 1637. Coins from this mint can be seen in Ceredigion Museum. Inside the seventeenth-century building James Thorburn found the remains of five clay-lined furnaces and lead waste products. It is very tempting to think that here was the site of Bushell's mint, but we must be cautious as we have found evidence for a lot of activity in the first half of the seventeenth century at different points around the castle, though none as closely related as this to the sorts of activity one would associate with a mint. Another piece of evidence that may favour the identification of the mint in this spot is the fact that we found remains of a later phase of seventeenth-century activity on the site, which must belong to the time of the Civil War and have ended in 1649.

The excavations of 1982/83 not only provided much more information about the history of the castle, but they also raised several unanswered questions. With these in mind another MSC scheme, supervised by Angela Davies, was begun in 1984. The first part of the dig concentrated on clearing the south corner and south-east side of the Outer Bailey. The whole surviving length of the outer face of the inner curtain-wall was exposed, including the south angle-tower. Two arched openings in the inner curtain just north of its junction with the angle-tower proved to be the outlets for latrines originally situated in alcoves off the wall-walk passages along the inner curtain. The work in the south-east bailey added to our knowledge of the landscaping of the site.

The second part of the dig, in 1985, produced some of the most important results so far. As the deposits were removed in the south angle of the Outer Bailey the foundations of a wall began to appear which continued the line of the inner curtain towards the outer curtain. Later digging in the tower showed that this was indeed the inner curtain. Clearly, the original plan of the castle did not envisage the construction of the south-west inner curtain-wall with its interval tower. The earlier find of the limekiln and its relationship with the inner curtain had already hinted at a complicated sequence of events in the early years of the castle. Importantly, we could now show that the first builders had not planned a concentric layout like that finally settled upon.

Further excavation of the angle-tower and the southern end of the hall revealed in 1982/83 showed an even more complicated sequence of events. At some stage in the construction of the south-east inner curtain it was decided to abandon the direct connection with the outer curtain. Whatever had been built was demolished and the wall levelled to its foundation course. The south-west inner curtain was then built with a round angle-tower constructed over part of the line of the demolished south-east inner curtain. There was a small round stair-turret giving access to its upper floors on the north side of the tower. Later it was decided to construct the large hall in the south corner of the Inner Bailey. In order to roof this satisfactorily it was necessary to modify the rear of the angle tower giving it a straight back wall and D-shaped interior, and at the same time demolishing the stair turret.

There are several possible historical occasions for these various changes of plan in the records of the late thirteenth century, but it is impossible to be sure exactly how these events and rebuildings are related.

The excavations also confirmed the two main phases of seventeenth-century activity identified elsewhere in the hall, one of an industrial nature possibly connected with the mint, the other of a military nature, as evidenced by the provision of a firing bench in the tower, and probably belonging to the Civil War.

The excavations in the tower came to an end in March 1986, and the remains in the area were duly consolidated and made available for public access. A new scheme, again supervised by Angela Davies, was begun in the south tower of the Great Gate in 1986/87. The main discovery in the lower chamber of the tower was that the first floor had been supported by an arcade sprung from two piers, roughly on the axis of the tower; this is an unusual feature in castle architecture. Much of the time of this dig was taken up with clearing dumps of rubble over the tower and elucidating the post-medieval activity on the site.

During the same scheme the excavators uncovered a rectangular medieval building behind the central tower of the south-west inner curtain. It had been built after the curtain, but how much later is uncertain. The uneven nature of the rock surface within it suggested that it had either been floored with timber at a higher level or it had never been floored properly, or even that the building had not been completed. The evidence did not allow us to choose between these possibilities.

The final MSC scheme on the site was supervised by Donald Stewart between July 1987 and October 1988. The original scheme envisaged finishing off in the south chamber of the Great Gate and full excavation of the north-east Outer Bailey, the north angle-tower of the inner curtain and the north corner of the Inner Bailey.

In the event, we were never able to get more than half the intended labour force, and activities were perforce curtailed in the interests of preserving the archaeology of the site. Nevertheless some very important additional information was gained about the history of the castle.

In the south chamber of the Great Gate, during renovation of the curving east wall, a vaulted chamber with a latrine was cleared of later rubble. The north-east inner curtain-wall was a disappointment. The rubble bank over it had suggested a much better state of preservation, but it proved to be largely demolished towards its northern end. However, just north of the angle made with the north tower of the Great Gate the excavators uncovered a well-preserved arched latrine outlet in the wall.

Inside the north-east inner curtain was a long narrow building with walls of stone in clay, which was entered by six doorways on the west. The structure had been erected over a thick deposit of seventeenth-century and earlier refuse.

The most probable explanation of the building was that it was a stable. Within it was one of the most startling discoveries of all the excavations – a skeleton of a young man laid in a shallow grave. How he died and how he came to be buried in that position can only be a matter for speculation; he was certainly interred just before the demolition of the castle in 1649 and not later.

Behind the north angle-tower the excavators uncovered two round-based ovens or kilns of the seventeenth century. Further south of these were the remains of another seventeenth-century building containing a smithying hearth. This feature was not fully excavated and it was re-covered to preserve it for further study.

The remains of the base of a semi-circular bastion were found about half-way along the outer face of the north-east curtain-wall. This belonged to the seventeenth century, presumably to the time of the Civil War. It is of particular interest not only for revealing something of the military arrangements at the castle at that time, but also for shedding light on the possible site of the medieval town wall of Aberystwyth. Its position suggests it may have been covering a perceived weak spot in the castle defences, possibly where the town wall approached and gave cover to attackers.

In a short essay such as this I have only been able to highlight some of the most important results of the research. For example, I have said very little about the wealth of medieval objects such as pottery, tiles, coins and metalwork discovered. Nevertheless, I hope the reader will appreciate just how greatly our knowledge of Aberystwyth Castle has been increased by the years of excavation. I must pay

*Aberystwyth Castle, 1988. The skeleton of a young man, probably buried at the time of the Civil War, just inside the north-east inner curtain-wall. (Crown Copyright, RCAHMW)*

tribute to the many people, colleagues, council employees and excavators that have made the research so pleasurable. The Commissioners of the Royal Commission have kindly agreed that the results will be published in 2004 as a detailed monograph, written by me, that I hope will do full justice to this important site of which the people of Aberystwyth can be justifiably proud.

*David M. Browne MA, FRAI, FRGS*

## A Lovely Little Village

'We have a lovely little village in Penparcau, and we can make a charming village of it.'[1] These were the words of Alderman C.M. Williams in August 1925 during a meeting of Aberystwyth Borough Council to discuss the 1924 Housing Act. Today the casual observer might be forgiven for disagreeing, at first glance, with Alderman Williams. The original village, standing alongside the A487 with its own shops, chapel, churches and school, has been dwarfed by the profusion of local authority housing estates which were built between 1927 and the mid 1970s, and again during the 1990s by the housing association, Tai Cantref. A glance at pre-1927 photographs of the village, however, would certainly substantiate the statement made by Alderman Williams over seventy-five years ago.

Penparcau, which over its long history has also been known as Penyparke, Penparciau and Penparke, has been home to members of my family continuously since at least 1885 and therefore holds a special place in my affections. It is overlooked by the Iron Age hill fort of Pen Dinas, crowned with the monument (erected in 1852) to commemorate the 1st Duke of Wellington, victor of Waterloo. The hill fort is one of the largest and most prominent in Wales and was built some 2,000 years ago as a tribal capital, its occupants holding sway over the surrounding landscape.

There had been very little building activity in the village during the nineteenth and early twentieth centuries. The majority of houses were low-roofed, whitewashed cottages with cob walls. These were mainly grouped around the Southgate tollhouse and at Back Street and Ty Cam, behind the present-day post office. Typically, these small cottages were overcrowded, providing accommodation for large families, which were a common feature of the time. Groups of up to twelve households would, if they were lucky, be served by one communal closet and one water tap and many of the cottages had no doors or windows at the rear.

*City Road, Pen Parke.*

*Penparcau.*

At the south end of the village stood the Southgate tollhouse, the name still used today, where originally five roads met. The tollhouse was built in 1770/71 by the Powell family of nearby Nanteos, and remained standing until 1964 when it was dismantled and reassembled at the Museum of Welsh Folk Life at St Fagan's near Cardiff. The last occupant, Mrs Kate Hopkins, who is still remembered in the village, lived in the toll house for thirty-nine years and was said, at the end of her occupation, to live in constant fear of accidents from the increasing road traffic which passed by on either side of her home. Until about 1910, a row of small cottages stood opposite the tollhouse, one of which had been an inn known as Piccadilly. The area of Penparcau now known as Southgate was still known in the 1970s as Piccadilly by many of the older residents in the village.

During the early years of the twentieth century villagers would knead their own bread and take it to the local shopkeeper, 'Ann y Bwlch Shop', every Tuesday for baking in large oval tins. Ann charged a penny for baking each loaf, and also made trays of treacle and oatcakes. Penparcau also had its fair share of local characters. Among these was Bonnor Jones, a boot maker and cobbler whose great love was music. Jones would always have his tuning pitchfork in the pocket of his leather apron. The village children would visit Jones in his workshop where they would run through the Sol-fa. The local tailor, Evan Morris, enjoyed photography in his spare time and was always willing to record family occasions and local events. Ann Rees was well known for addressing every person she met by their Christian name and their surname, no matter how well she knew them!

Much of the land in and around Penparcau was owned by the Nanteos estate, which provided many of the villagers with employment. Children at the village school would often be invited to Nanteos for afternoon teas and the annual prize-giving would always be held at the mansion. Colonel William Powell MP, known as 'the General', would always entertain the children in the full dress uniform of the

*Penparcau, mid-1900s.*

Royal Cardiganshire Militia, of which he was Commanding Officer. The Powell family had lived at Nanteos since 1698, although the present house, thought to be the finest example of Georgian architecture in Mid Wales, dates from 1739. The Powells became one of the most influential and powerful families in the county, their estate extending to some 30,000 acres, including lead mines and large parts of the town of Aberystwyth. The family provided MPs, High Sheriffs, Justices of the Peace and a Lord Lieutenant to the county. The Powells were also Lords of the Manor of Llanbadarn Fawr, which gave them extensive feudal manorial rights, which they continued to exercise until the middle of the twentieth century. Until the 1940s, every year on Boxing Day, the villagers would walk the short distance to the mansion where the Gogerddan Hounds and Nanteos Harriers would be gathered for the most important

meet of the Hunt year. Food, ale and merriment were in abundance as the villagers watched the elite of county society, led by the Powells and their kinsmen, the Pryse family, indulge in one of their favourite sports. However, the fortunes of the estate were dealt a fatal blow when in November 1918, a few days before the armistice, the nineteen-year-old heir, William Edward George Pryse Wynne Powell, was shot dead by a German sniper. The Celtic cross at Southgate was unveiled in 1922 as a memorial to him. His father, Edward Powell, died in 1930 leaving a widow, Margaret, to uphold the family traditions until her death in 1952. The estate, by now little more than 2,000 acres, passed to distant relatives before being broken up and sold off in 1967.

Another landowner in the village was the barrister John Maurice Davies, who lived at Plas Antaron (which is now a hotel), during

*Penparcau, 1930. The first houses were built in Penparcau in 1927.*

the 1870s. Mr Davies is remembered for the peculiar names he gave two of his daughters: Agnes Undecim and Rosea Ultima. The row of large houses leading to Crugiau farm and Rhyd y Felin hill is named Antaron Avenue. Antaron is one of the oldest names in the area and is mentioned as the site of a battle in the *Brut y Tywysogion* (Chronicle of the Princes), written in the eleventh century by the monks of Llanbadarn Fawr and Ystrad Fflur (Strata Florida).

The spiritual needs of the villagers were catered for by both the chapel and the church. Ebenezer Calvinistic Methodist chapel, which nestles between the Spar and the Co-op on Penparcau Road, was built in 1848 as a branch of Aberystwyth's Tabernacle in Mill Street. It was the custom for a member of Ebenezer's congregation to walk to Aberystwyth on a Sunday morning to escort the minister to Penparcau. The chapel was rebuilt in 1939 and today has a thriving congregation and Sunday school. The Church in Wales is present in the congregation of St Anne's church, which, in the past, has had a well-known amateur dramatic society. Recently, a new parish hall adjoining the church has been opened and is available for use by the community as a whole. In 1970 Welsh Martyrs' church was opened in Piercefield Lane to tend to the needs of local Roman Catholics. The first Mass was held in August 1970 followed by the dedication by Bishop Petit in the following October. Previously, Mass had been celebrated in Penparcau since 1952 in Neuadd Goffa, the memorial hall which had been opened in October 1928 and which has recently been extensively refurbished. The former Methodist church in Maesmaelor is now a meeting house for the Quakers, while the Methodists worship in the former Kingdom Hall of Jehovah's Witnesses in Ty Cam.

Penparcau School was built in 1846 at the top of Pen y Bont Hill under the patronage of Elizabeth and Martha Pritchard, natives of Shrewsbury who had settled in Aberystwyth. One of the best-remembered schoolmasters was George Hunt Thomas, known as Thomas Penparcau, who had previously been a mariner. Among the subjects Thomas taught were trigonometry, geometry and navigation and the Board of Education reports on the school were always excellent. Thomas retired from the school in 1884, two years before his death. In addition to paying visits to Nanteos, the children would often be provided with treats on visits to the nearby Glanpaith and Tan y Bwlch mansions. The original school building has recently been renovated and converted into housing, having in the past been used as a carpet centre and a shop. The present school buildings are situated on the opposite side of the road, below Southgate.

As Aberystwyth expanded, so did the need to provide housing for the town's growing population. In 1926 the borough council purchased a 14.2-acre field known as Cae Ffynnon, on sloping ground between the A487 and the Afon Rheidol, from Captain Edward Powell of Nanteos. A mix of ninety two- and three-bedroomed houses was built between 1927 and 1935. In 1935 the council sought further land in Penparcau and set its sights on the 8-acre Seaton's field lying directly opposite Cae Ffynnon on the lower slopes of Pen Dinas. Despite protracted negotiations with the Nanteos estate, a price could not be agreed and a compulsory purchase order was made. Work commenced in 1939 on the eighty houses, which became known as Maesheli. House building was suspended during the Second World War, but recommenced in late 1947 when 21 acres of land belonging to Nanteos at Plas Helyg, Piercefield Lane and Cae Tase were again the subject of compulsory purchase. The houses were completed in the early 1950s and became known as Maesmaelor (built on Cae Tase), Plas Helyg, Heol y Garth, Heol Nanteos and Heol y Wern (which were built at Piercefield). Between 1952 and 1974, the council developed some sixty acres of land at Pen y Bont with a mixture of flats and houses being built. In recent years, housing development has also taken place at Cae Job on the slopes of Pen Dinas above Piercefield Farm and at Crugiau Farm, Southgate.

Penparcau can claim to have its own ghost, the Headless Dog of Penparcau, which has many similarities to the well-known legend of Bedd Gelert. According to the legend, the young daughter of a sheep farmer became ill during the lambing season. The farmer decided to ride into town to fetch a doctor and while he was away he entrusted his daughter and newborn lambs to the care of his faithful dog. On the farmer's return with the doctor, they were faced with the sight of his daughter lying savaged and the lambs having had their heads torn off. In his anger the farmer, believing his bloodied dog to be the culprit, struck off the dog's head. Eventually, the daughter made a full recovery and was able to tell her father what had happened. A large wild beast had attacked and killed the lambs and would surely have killed her had the faithful dog not fended off the wild creature. According to the legend, the ghost of the Headless Dog of Penparcau roams the slopes of Pen Dinas after dark during the lambing season.

My own childhood memories of Penparcau are happy ones. As children we would spend many hours on Pen Dinas, never tiring of picking blackberries, sliding down the numerous slopes on flattened cardboard boxes and playing endless games of hide and seek. With its magnificent views of Bae Ceredigion, Aberystwyth and the surrounding countryside, Pen Dinas is still a place I never tire of. Each school morning the minibus would collect the small band of children from Seaton's Corner opposite Mr Taravella's, the Penparcau butcher, and ferry us to St Padarn's School. Having later moved on to Ysgol Penweddig, we would walk, via Pont Sant Brieuc footbridge, to Llanbadarn Road each morning and return along the same route after school. In the early evenings and at weekends much of my spare time would be spent with my grandfather delivering milk around Penparcau, as did my father and his brothers and sisters in their youth. My grandfather, Robert Gorman, who lived in Maesheli, was well known in Penparcau and was affectionately referred to as 'Jock the Milk' by the many people who knew him. During one or two periods of heavy snowfall, various family members would turn out to help ensure that customers received their milk, which often had to be delivered on foot because of the weather conditions.

There have been many changes in the village, even in recent years: new housing, the loss of the village playing fields to make way for a roundabout, road improvements and the closure of Southgate Service Station (or Top Shop, as it was known to villagers). Here, petrol would be dispensed the old fashioned way by one of the two brothers who owned the business. When I was a very young child, there was no sign of the mass of houses, which now occupy the hillside behind the present day school. A wooded track, the remains of which are still visible, wound its way from behind the school to Tyn y Fron farmhouse that now stands, somewhat out of place, amongst the houses of Heol Tyn y Fron.

Throughout its long history, Penparcau has always been a lively and busy community, which has managed to retain something of its Welsh identity and of the charm referred to by Alderman Williams in 1925. The many voluntary groups, organizations and societies which flourish in the village continue to foster a sense of community for residents both young and old in what is now one of the largest settlements in Ceredigion.

[1] Jones, P.E. Council House Building in Aberystwyth, 1900-1974, in Journal of the Ceredigion Antiquarian Society, 1997.

*David Gorman*

## Llanbadarn Fawr

Llanbadarn Fawr is situated approximately one mile away from the town of Aberystwyth on the west coast of Wales. This small village is dominated by the huge church of St Padarn, situated in the middle of the village. Llanbadarn Fawr means 'Great church of St Padarn' and is evidence of how important the church is to the village.

### St Padarn
There are three main sources about St Padarn available. Rhygyfarch in *The Life of David* writes the earliest reference to him, in AD 1097 (in reference to St David), thought to be about 500 years after he lived. There is another reference written in around 1100 by an unknown author, in the margin of a copy of St Augustine's treatise *De Trinitate*. This reference is drawn from a poem and states that there were many traditions in Llanbadarn Fawr at this time. It also speaks of the importance of St Padarn and discusses the great affection felt for him by the local people. The other main reference is 'The Story of the life of St Padarn' in the British Museum manuscript *Lives of Celtic Saints*, compiled about 1200 by monks in Mid Wales.

According to 'The Story of the life of St Padarn' he was born in Armorica (Letavia, Brittany) and was the son of Petron and Gueon and was of noble birth. It is said that Petron abandoned his wife and son to go to Britain to learn more of religion. Later in life Padarn left as well to go to Britain in search of his father; he travelled in the company of three monks who soon appointed him their leader.

Upon reaching the coast of Wales they travelled from Gwent to the west coast. By the time St Padarn had reached the current site of Llanbadarn Fawr he had more than 800 people in his group; they all settled in what was to become Llanbadarn Fawr. There are no other churches called St Padarn in this script, but it is possible that there were others.

There are two main stories noted in the British Museum manuscript that should be mentioned. The first details a confrontation with Maelgwn regarding land. Maelgwn landed on Clarach beach looking for Deheubarth, trying to find an excuse to plunder the land. He came across St Padarn and as a token of loyalty he gave to him some hampers filled with all of his treasure. However, when the group finally reached Llanbadarn Fawr Maelgwn demanded the hampers back, when they were opened they discovered that they were full of moss and gravel. Maelgwn flew into a rage and

*Llanbadarn Fawr, c. 1880.*

claimed that St Padarn had stolen from him. St Padarn himself had not disturbed the hampers and said that everyone in the group, both his men and Maelgwn's, should place their hands into a container of boiling water. Those whose hands had indeed touched the hampers would be scalded. The men of St Padarn did so and their hands came out unhurt; however, when the men of Maelgwn did so their hands were scalded and so Maelgwn could argue no further, and left.

Another story of the saint's greatness takes place soon after this one. An angel bade St David to take St Padarn with him to Jerusalem to be consecrated by Bishops of the Patriarch, where St Padarn was given a tunic. Following on from this story there is another, this one concerned with a 'tyrant called Arthur' who according to *The Life of David* insisted that the tunic given to St Padarn was actually his by right. St Padarn refused to hand over the tunic and so

Arthur stormed out and was instantly swallowed by the earth. Only when he apologized (and meant it) was he released. This particular incident is also documented in the British Museum manuscript.

It is said that St Padarn spent twenty-one years in Wales altogether: seven years in Llanbadarn at the mother church, seven in Angrams Cross and seven in another church of unknown location. However, it is improbable that exactly seven years were spent in each.

St Padarn returned to Letavia to see to some unrest but this trip proved fatal and he died on 15 April. After his death the country's problems worsened greatly and this was blamed on the death of St Padarn and also on the theft of his relics. He was buried in the city of Guenet, Letavia.

There are several saints named Padarn (Patern or Paternus) recorded in the fifth century and there is confusion between them. It is therefore very hard to get an

87

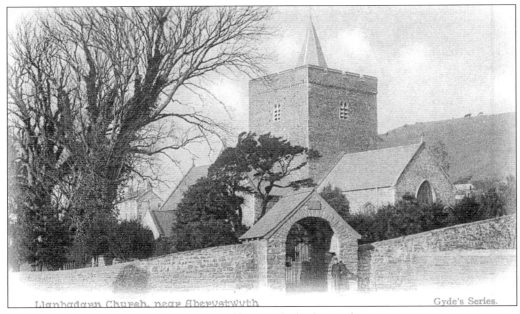

Llanbadarn Church, near Aberystwyth. Gyde's Series.

*Llanbadarn church – note the absence of buildings in the background.*

*The church entrance.*

exact date of our St Padarn's first arrival in Wales. There is only one reference to a St Padarn in the genealogical table of Welsh Saints (known as Banedd y Saint, compiled in the thirteenth century) but this gives a very different parentage and pedigree to the St Padarn in the British Museum manuscript. The Welsh historian Sir John Edward Lloyd thought this pedigree was more probable than the one outlined in the British Museum manuscript. In Banedd y Saint his parentage makes him second cousin to Cadfan of Towyn, Tydecho of Mawddwy and Trino of Flandrinio. He was the son of Pedarn (or Petronius) and the grandson of Emyr Llydou, hence giving him Welsh ancestry.

According to A *Topographical Dictionary of Wales*, compiled by Samuel Lewis in 1833, Llanbadarn Fawr was anciently called Llanbadarn Gaerog or 'Walled Llanbadarn'. Lewis goes on to record that St Padarn studied under Iltutus at Llantwit Major. After St Padarn was recalled to Letavia, where he died, the church was called 'Paternensis' in his memory; this is recorded in the minutes of the Synod held in the County of Worcester in AD 601.

It is important for the reader to note that everything that has been written about St Padarn was written long after his death. It should also be noted that there was also a St Padarn in England at the same time. *The Life of St. Padarn* written in 1120 is very complex and is thought to muddle the Welsh St Padarn with the English one.

### St Padarn's church

The church marks the most northerly penetration of St Padarn; there are as previously mentioned two other churches that were founded by him. This church, unlike the others, was not founded as a retreat but as a place of public worship and a centre of Christianity. The church has a cruciform plan with a massive central tower and central spire that dominates the village. In the Middle Ages it was the was the largest church in the largest parish in Wales.

This church was the first in the Aberystwyth area; the second was St Michael's, behind the Old College in the town. The second church was required as the position of Llanbadarn made it hard for the elderly or infirm residents of Aberystwyth to travel to church to worship.

When the Normans arrived the church was placed under the rule of St Benedict and its lands were given to the Benedictine abbey of St Peter in Gloucester. A cell of the main house in Gloucester was built in Llanbadarn. In 1135 the Normans lost their hold on this part of Wales and Gerald of Wales records that with the removal of their rule the Benedictines were removed from Llanbadarn and the Celtic monks reclaimed their possessions.

Between 1188 and 1247 there is no mention of the monastery in the records. In 1245 King Henry III recovered northern

*The churchyard at Llanbadarn, early 1900s.*

*Llanbadarn church before restoration.*

Ceredigion and retained control of the territory for eleven years; the current church was built during this period. During the mid-thirteenth century the rights of St Padarn's monastery lapsed and passed to the Crown; however, it is very unlikely that those appointed to run the site by the king actually came to Llanbadarn, as they would have employed local Welshmen to do the work. One of the most famous men associated with Llanbadarn was Thomas Bradwordine who was rector in the Middle Ages; he later became Archbishop of Canterbury.

The nineteenth century saw the start of extensive renovation work on the church. The restorers took down the covered screens that according to Mayrick in his description of the church in *The History and Antiquities of Cardigan* (1810) were used to separate the chapel and the north transept from the rest of the church. Mayrick believed that the screens had actually been present since about the time of Henry VIII.

The restoration began in earnest in 1868 and lasted for several years. It was carried out by John Pollard Seddon and his partner Prichard, who also worked on Llandaff Cathedral. There are some architectural features shared by the two buildings. At some point before 1868 the roof had been replaced, during which work the walls had been extensively damaged. Seddon took down and replaced most of the walls and raised the roof to its original height. All the ceilings of the church are of a good design and the roof especially highlights the mediaeval quality of the church. During this work the present-day pews were also installed. The church walls were restored once more in 1934 and the north transept was converted to use as a chapel in 1935.

Recently restoration has begun on the church bells. The plan is to replace the old frame and to this end, bells and frame were removed earlier this year (2001). The bells have been recast using the originals as models.

Throughout the centuries St Padarn's has remained one of the mother churches of

Wales, a constant hive of activity through worship and service that still continues today. On Sundays the service is said in both English and Welsh.

*Miss R. J. Phillips*

## The Ancestors

Exactly when the first settlers arrived in the area we now call Aberystwyth is something we will never know. However, during the twentieth century, with the aid of science and dedicated field-work, archaeologists have learnt much about the homes and lives of the ancient people of Wales. Even so, this is only a fragment of what we would like to know about those people who lived in and around our neighbourhood so many years ago.

Although we are using the Iron Age period as our starting block, we must remember people had lived here for thousands of years, long before the first use of metals like bronze and iron. Flint workings found on the lower west side of Pen Dinas provide evidence of human activity here around 7,000-8,000 years ago, during what is known as the Mesolithic era.

Until the Roman invasion of Britain, little was recorded of the history of this country, leaving us with hardly any knowledge of the lives and culture of the Iron Age people here. Fortunately the Celtic tribes of central and southern Europe were well documented by the Greeks and Romans.

Therefore we can merely try to visualize the scene of some 2,300 years ago and hope that the results will reflect as true a picture as possible, yet leave some room for consideration and debate. Firstly we must

*Showing tribal divisions in late Iron Age.*

clear our minds of that which we see in and around Aberystwyth today. For instance, of the roads, houses and shops, nothing man-made that exists today existed at that time, other than the now buried remains of the fort on Pen Dinas. In order to try to understand the environment in which these people lived, we have to bear in mind that the geography has altered significantly over hundreds of years. Advancements in agricultural methods have changed our farmlands and the construction of roads and buildings has completely altered the landscape and continues to do so.

If we try to visualize the area in the Iron Age we would see both the Ystwyth and Rheidol valleys as wet marshy areas, with willow and marsh plants occupying the low areas, especially near the estuaries. Apart from those very wet lands near the rivers much of the land in these spacious valleys was probably well cultivated, but to what extent would have depended on the density of the population. It has been established

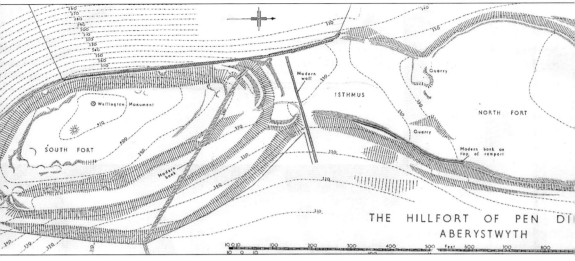

*Hillfort at Pen Dinas. (RCAHMW Crown Copyright)*

that, apart from Pen Dinas, there were other settlements in the area. Indeed, the settlements in the Iron Age landscape were more numerous and varied in type than we have previously imagined.

It was once a strongly held view that the people who constructed the hill-fort on Pen Dinas came here by immigration but I, along with many others today, believe this community already resided here and, for their protection, decided to build and occupy the fortress on the hill.

The construction of the fortified settlement was started around 300 BC. In choosing the location the area would have been well surveyed. As well as the defensive aspect, the availability of water, building material like quarry stone, and the quality of the land for agricultural purposes would have been taken into account before the final decision was made. The builders found the hill site attractive, as it was a natural safe haven with two ideal harbours in the river estuaries.

It would help to look at the construction

of the dwellings and defences on Pen Dinas, as revealed during the excavations of the site during the period 1933-1937 under the direction of Professor D. Forde. The report of this makes interesting reading; see Excavations at Pen Dinas, Aberystwyth, published by the Royal Commission on Ancient and Historical Monuments, Aberystwyth. The fortress is in two parts, now known as North Fort and South Fort. The former covered 4 acres and the latter roughly 5 acres. The two parts were joined by parallel ramparts and it was here on the eastern side that the main gate was situated. It is believed that the northern half of the fort was the first to be constructed.

The South Fort had only one rampart on its west and south sides, as here the hillside is very steep and this was considered a sufficient defence. An attack would have been difficult to mount from these steep slopes. The arduous building work probably involved the whole of the able-bodied population. The job of carrying baskets of soil and rubble onto the ramparts may even have fallen to the women and older children. In some parts oxen and sledges would have been used to cart soil, dug from the ditches, onto the rampart top. The oxen would also be necessary for hauling boulders and stone from the river and hillside quarries to face the ramparts, especially around the gateways. Pointed timber poles were fixed on top of the embankment to form the palisade and were built in as work progressed.

The gates must have been very robust and hung on strong hinges. Great care was taken over this part of the defences as the gate could be the weakest part, being vulnerable to fire should an enemy decide on this method of attack.

Finally, the dwelling and store-houses on Pen Dinas were either circular or D-shaped in construction, with a shallow drainage ditch dug across the floor. The walls were most likely formed from strong upright timbers, closely set, which were interwoven with wattle and rendered with mud or clay. A heavy central pole supported the roof which was thatched with rushes and covered in turf for protection from high winds. For the same reason, the roof was large and extended to near ground level. It was previously assumed that a hole in the roof would have been left as an exit for smoke, but the Iron Age experiment at Castell Henllys, Pembrokeshire, proved it caused draught, so it was decided it was an impractical feature and would probably not have been adopted. The dwelling-houses measured some 6m or more across, with a raised section on one side used as seating by day and as a sleeping place at night. The hearth was a hollow about 45cm in diameter in the floor and a fire was probably kept burning continuously. There would have been little light because of the absence of windows and the smoke-laden atmosphere,

*Fencing against the stock.*

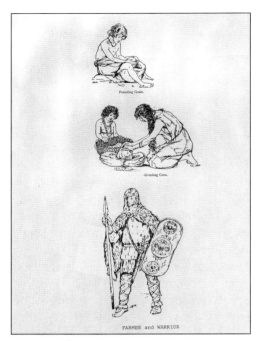

*Farmer and warrior.*

involved the cutting down of woods in ever increasing circles, putting great pressure on the wild game. However, this was balanced by the cultivation of the cleared land, enabling the settlers on the hill, possibly a population of around 150, to become more independent as they satisfied their needs through agriculture. Only a few cattle would have been kept through winter, retained for breeding, ploughing and haulage work. Any horses would surely have been kept outside most of the winter, perhaps getting shelter at night in rough weather. On the other hand, the hardy sheep would fend for themselves, and would have been kept in large numbers, supplying meat, wool and skins. It is debatable whether pigs were kept in the village as they would have consumed a lot of grain in winter. Grain was an important requirement for both the settlers and their stock. Producing grain involves ploughing and much hard labour. As land under the plough is land lost to grazing, we must visualize only a comparatively small arable acreage.

although the smoke permeating the thatch must have discouraged the vermin.

The excavations did not reveal any trace of grain storage pits. Possibly the grain was stored in purpose-built huts, of rectangular construction and built on stilts in order to keep out rodents and avoid dampness. Dogs, housed under the granary at night, would have also helped to keep any unwanted visitors away.

Having lightly covered the subject of construction we now turn to the people and their lives. Although their housing and environment may seem primitive in some sense compared to our modern way of life, we should not underestimate the resourcefulness and intelligence of these people as we try to recapture something of their lives.

As time passed, the increasing demands for timber used in building and fuel

The job of tending the animals would have fallen on the women and children, with the children watching over the stock in the grazing areas by day and returning them to their enclosures at night. We can be sure dogs were used to work the stock by day and also acted as sentries at night, giving warning of intruders, human or otherwise. Other sources of food were available, fish being plentiful in the bay, but regular catches could not be relied on, unless netting was practised. The rivers were an easier source, with salmon and sewin travelling in large numbers upriver to the spawning grounds from spring till autumn. We can see that high protein food was available but whether the diet was balanced is uncertain. There was possibly a shortage of vegetables, although herbs, vetches and beans, as well as wild onions (which grow even today on the slopes below the National Library, Aberystwyth) may have helped balance any deficiency.

Baking was done in a simple clay oven and bread was made with wheat or rye flour and probably risen by wild yeast. We cannot help but speculate on what they drank in addition to milk and water; for instance, did they have an alcoholic drink? If so, perhaps it would have been a strong real ale sweetened with honey and flavoured with herbs, then left to ferment before being drunk.

Having dealt briefly with the essentials of life such as food, drink and shelter, we look to clothing which we know was produced on Pen Dinas after the discovery of two spindlewhorls and two loom weights. The main garment was a plaid, which resembled a cloak. This was wrapped around the body in cold weather and at night served as a blanket, often worn over one shoulder and secured by a brooch. Both males and females wore a type of belted smock and leggings of fur. Of course clothing would vary with the seasons, but certainly a lot of wool was used and was dyed in bright colours. Leather and hide were produced for belts, trappings and shoes. Most of what they required was made in the village. The blacksmith worked iron to make tools and utensils, whilst the carpenter was also a very important man doing most jobs around the fort. Pottery was another craft undertaken and although little has been found, a reproduction of the Malvern jar found on the site is exhibited in Aberystwyth town museum.

At this time considerable trade was taking place throughout the country. Iron, livestock, clothing and pottery – in fact most goods – were tradeable. The centre of all these activities was the main settlement on the hill, ruled by a tribal chief at its head, elders as council, and maybe a druid, who was a powerful man overseeing all religious events, such as marriage, death and perhaps even sacrifices, to pacify their gods. People were affected by illness then just as they are today and he would treat them with herbs, casting spells as though to remove the evil spirit. The patient would then recover naturally, or be called to the gods, probably prematurely!

The people, although farmers, were also warriors and their lives were governed by their environment and the need for survival. Throughout history weapons have played an important part in the life of mankind. The inhabitants of the fort would have needed weapons to defend themselves, but there was more to it than that, as weapons also represented wealth. The more the output from the land, the more weapons that could be acquired and the more secure they would feel. Also weapons themselves were very tradeable.

The Roman invasion of southern England by Julius Caesar in 55 BC possibly went unnoticed on the west coast of Wales, but it was the later invasion by the Romans in AD 43 which eventually affected the local people here. It is believed that the people had by this time left the hill and were well dispersed around the area. After many years the Romans eventually established order throughout Wales. There is no indication that the local population was ever in conflict with them. Peace and stability allowed the local population to expand and prosper, with their lives now to change for ever.

Work was available on road building, in the mines and also as tradesmen, who were in great demand. For example blacksmiths, carpenters and many others found work in the service of the Romans, including enlistment into the army itself. Coinage is likely to have been in circulation at this time and used alongside the barter system of the locals as added trade and work increased. Many Roman coins have been found locally and although the Romans never resided in Aberystwyth itself, they had forts as near as Capel Bangor and Trawscoed which added a lot of employment, trade and influence locally, particularly through agriculture. Many farmers would have been involved in the selective breeding of stronger and larger war ponies for the cavalry based there, and the Army's requirements for fodder, meat and grain must have been substantial. At this time the central government took land and created many farms which were managed by Romanized British farmers. Many spoke Latin as well as their native language.

Unfortunately stability and security was not to last and with trouble raging throughout the Roman Empire and against Rome itself, the army was recalled after 400 years, with Britain left to look to its own defences. As we talk of progress with the passage of time, one would expect that with so much stone in the district that the population's huts would have been replaced by homes of more substantial construction and they would have been influenced by the presence of Roman architecture in the district. Sadly there is no evidence to support this view, as no such example has survived the rigours of time.

I have through these few pages tried to understand and visualize the lives and ways of the early Aberystwyth people. The fact we do not have any written record makes it difficult but nevertheless interesting, as it gives us the opportunity of using our imagination on the subject. Furthermore it is doubtful if you will ever again pass through Penparcau without glancing up at Pen Dinas, and – who knows – one day you may even climb it, to see the former home of these early Aberystwyth ancestors.

*John Barrett*

## *Kaleidoscopic Aberystwyth*

Aberystwyth has had a number of guises. At first it was a medieval borough, then the focus shifted to its function as a port. Later it attracted wealthy tourists and, soon after, the less privileged holidaymaker visited the town. From the end of the nineteenth century to the present day, the town has emerged as a cultural and educational centre. These changes have been chronicled by a succession of travel writers who, while visiting the town, have attempted to condense Aberystwyth into words. In 1188 Gerald of Wales visited Llanbadarn Fawr, nearly a century before Aberystwyth itself was founded by Edward I in 1277. Gerald was not impressed by the 'wicked people' he saw there. We cherish the record he provided, and we should also value those of later visitors to Aberystwyth, a place Gerald could not visit because it did not then exist.

The next individual to travel through Wales and write an account of the journey was the chaplin and librarian to Henry VIII, John Leland, between the years 1535 and 1543. Aberystwyth impressed Leland, although his description is very sparing: 'Abreostuthe hath been waullyd, and hathe greate privilegis, and is better market than Cairdigan.'

This comparison between the two foremost towns in the county is an early recognition of, and contribution to, a rivalry that would continue for centuries. Later historical accounts also tend to compare the towns. The depiction of Aberystwyth by John Taylor in 1652 is less flattering. He considers it 'to be a miserable market town' and is disappointed to see piles of rubble after the destruction of the castle by gunpowder in the Civil War. However, he indicates the wealth of the town's hinterland when he writes 'within four miles of this town are the silver mines'.

The reduction of the castle to ruins has unfortunately also reduced interest in its exciting past. Sir Richard Colt Hoare, who translated Gerald of Wales's *Journey through Wales* and *Description of Wales*, thought the remains of the castle were 'very trifling' when he passed through in 1796. This view is repeated in succeeding centuries by Black's *Tourist's Guide to Wales*, 1881 and by Wales, *The Rough Guide* in 1998. One American visitor celebrates its dilapidated condition because it liberates the town from the memory of past subjugation.

That wealth hinted at by Taylor was to transform Aberystwyth into a noteworthy port, although lead not silver would be the main export. A number of visitors report coal being exported despite there being no coal mines in the vicinity. One of these is Daniel Defoe: 'This town is enriched by the coals and lead which is found in the neighbourhood and is a populous, but a very dirty black smoaky place, and we fancy'd the people looked as if they liv'd continually in the coal or lead mines.'

This image sounds like the Rhondda in the nineteenth century, but it is Defoe's impression of Aberystwyth in the mid-1720s. Far from being a vibrant place, most historians regard Aberystwyth as suffering in the first half of the eighteenth century as the result of stagnation in the lead industry. Maps produced at the time indicate little development of the town since Tudor times. Defoe goes on to note that despite the appearance of the people, 'they are rich and the place populous.' Perhaps Defoe's description of a bustling town was the result of having travelled along the relatively peaceful route from St David's beforehand.

In 1795 Joseph Hucks and his companion, Samuel Taylor Coleridge, also commented on Aberystwyth's port: 'The trade is not by any means contemptible; great quantities of coal and lead are found in the neighbourhood and shipped from this port to different parts of England.'

Again there is the strange reference to coal. Possibly the authors thought the coal imported from Neath and Deeside was being exported. When Hucks visited Aberystwyth the town was expanding. Trade was stimulated by the location of the Customs House in the town in 1763. Previously most of the lead had been exported via Aberdovey. Some visitors were less impressed by the town's economy. A year after Huck's description, Hoare remarked that there was 'very little trade except lime and slate.' However, the most significant decline came during the nineteenth century. The Yorkshireman E.R. Horsfall-Turner, in his guide to the county of around 1902, wrote that 'at the beginning of Victoria's reign it was the third port in Wales [but now it is] greatly diminished.'

Towards the end of the eighteenth century Aberystwyth began to attract holidaymakers who stayed in the town rather than merely travelled through. The interest in seaside holidays among the better off can be traced to Dr Richard Russell's book in 1750 extolling the medicinal benefits of sea bathing. Hoare, who praised

Aberystwyth's bathing facilities in 1796, is critical in 1802. He describes some additions to the town since his last visit, such as new houses, a new bridge across the Rheidol and paving in the town. The beach, however was 'pebbly and irksome to walk upon.' He concludes by comparing Aberystwyth unfavourably with Tenby: 'The two places cannot in any respect bear a comparison either for beauty, convenience of bathing, or the luxuries of the table.'

A young woman, Catherine Hutton, wrote letters to a friend in 1787 during her holiday in Aberystwyth. In the main, she agrees with Hoare, especially about the quality of food in the town. The veal was 'abominable', the beef 'unavailable' and the ducks and geese tasted 'fishy'. Moreover, she is irritated by 'the common people [who]

complain that the sea bathers have raised the provision to an enormous price.' Although she attended two balls and attracted two suitors she wrote that she never wished to see Aberystwyth again.

Despite these critics, Aberystwyth did have a supporter in the antiquarian B.H. Malkin who wrote after visiting in 1803 that 'the town itself though generally represented in the tours and directories as irregular and dirty, appeared to me rather above than below the level of Welsh towns in general. It is much frequented as a bathing place, especially by Shropshire and Herefordshire families.' He could have also mentioned that theatre performances were held in the town from the 1780s.

It would, however, take more than plays and bathing to make the town comfortable

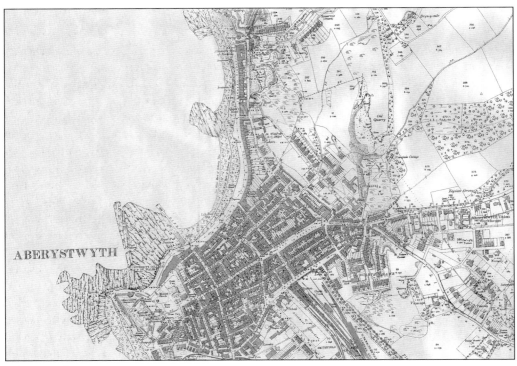

*Aberystwyth, c. 1904.*

*Punch and Judy show.*

for visitors. Although H. Wigstead had coined the description the 'Brighton of Wales' in 1797, the resort could only live up to it once suitable accommodation was provided. More quality accommodation was available after the development of Marine Terrace, which began in 1800 and can be seen on John Wood's map of 1835. But the improvement in lodgings did not silence all complaints about the town. The Revd Romilly wrote an entry in his diary on Sunday 27 August 1837 complaining about the difficulty in preaching in St Michael's church during stormy weather. His criticisms did not, however, extend to Cambridge House where he stayed.

Another vicar, the Revd John Evans, who passed through the town in 1803, was surprised to find the lodgings here cost as much as Weymouth. He also noted 'a number of fashionables' in the town.

Popularity as a resort no doubt deterred those travellers who wanted to experience 'natural' Wales. Thomas de Quincy, on the first recorded camping holiday in 1802, and George Borrow some fifty years later, did not visit Aberystwyth. In many travellers' opinion a fashionable town visited by such worthies as Sir Robert Peel MP paled in comparison with the antiquarian attractions inland. B.H. Malkin was one of the first to make this observation when he noted that the two ways to reach Cardigan were 'either along the coast, or through the interior of the county by Tregaron. The former is nearest by many miles, but the latter presents objects of more interest.'

Borrow met a young man in Esgyrn Hirion who told him: 'I came from Aberystwyth four months ago very unwell and am now perfectly recovered. I do not believe there is a healthier spot in all

Wales.' So it appears those seeking health in Aberystwyth at the time were in the wrong place. However, later on Borrow, while in the Ystwyth valley, calls it a 'lovely town', although he only mentions the 'still proud and commanding [castle] even in its ruins.' This is in keeping with his appreciation of the romantic above the modern and echoes an earlier visitor, Samuel R. Meyrick, who thought the castle had a 'most romantic appearance' in his survey of Cardiganshire published in 1810.

With the arrival of the railway in 1864, Aberystwyth attracted more tourists. Places of popular entertainment such as John James Hall, Market Hall and Temperance Hall sprouted in the 1870s. In 1865, three years after Borrow's *Wild Wales* was first published, Aberystwyth pier was opened. The change of name from Newfoundland Street to Bath Street in 1880s succinctly illustrates the town's shift away from port to resort. As well as these official name changes, people began unofficially to rename Aberystwyth. Wirt Sikes described the town in 1883 as 'the Newport [Rhode Island, USA] of Wales.' He also describes the dual nature of the town: 'It is a town of some importance, quite aside from its watering place character – thickly populated, bustling, and ancient of aspect as to its back streets, however, modern and merry in its sea-facing features.'

A traveller in 1848 conveys a similar impression of a busy town. On market day the market place and the neighbouring streets were full of people. Indeed the observer notes the enthusiasm of the traders as verging on the suicidal as they stand in the middle of the road promoting their wares. Later, the writer sees similar frantic activity in Machynlleth. In both towns it is the women who are identified as being the

most vigorous in the search for bargains. The market left more of an impression on the diarist than the watering-place attractions, although a point is made of saying how much the town's facilities had improved in recent years.

Later, in the Edwardian period ('the heyday of the staying visitors'), Aberystwyth acquired another unofficial title, 'the Biarritz of Wales.' Some travel writers disliked the increasingly commercial Aberystwyth of the time. S. Baring-Gould praised Tregaron, which he thought 'A pleasanter centre for excursions than Aberystwyth, partly because of its elevation, [but] mainly because there one is clear of the tripper.'

From this time onwards the popularity of Aberystwyth, among those travellers who publish accounts of their journey, is tarnished by this association with the 'masses'. Walter Wilkinson, who toured Wales with his puppet show after the Second World War, is astonished by the common folk's tolerance of a rain-soaked summer holiday. Others simply virtually ignore the town. One example is A.G. Bradley's *The Romance of Wales* published in 1929. In 270 pages there are two references to Aberystwyth, neither more than two lines long. Another traveller who overlooks the town is W.T. Palmer in the early 1930s. He is only interested in 'least known Wales', those places which are unsullied by the rail network with New Quay being his favourite.

Yet Aberystwyth's fourth incarnation, that of cultural centre, which happened at about the same time as the commercial growth, tempered criticism. Those who trembled at the sight of a pleasure-seeking tourist also praised Aberystwyth by calling it the 'Athens of Wales'. The college that was founded in 1872 became a university college

*Aberystwyth College, founded 1872, became a University College in 1893.*

in 1893 and there has been consistent praise for the college in accounts over the years. In the chapter 'The Devil's Bridge', E.M. Wilmot-Buxton praises the college's mixed sex teaching. Although the author is mistaken in the belief that Aberystwyth was the first to do this, it was significant that in 1909, three years before the book was published, Aberystwyth had more female students than male.

Thomas Firbank applauds the Welsh Plant Breeding Station, established as a research department of the college in 1919, in his 1953 book *A Country of Memorable Honour*. He shares the optimism expressed in the late 1930s that the ideas emanating from this department 'may prove revolutionary in the history of Wales' by improving the quality of upland grass. About twenty years on, Trevor Fishlock congratulates Aberystwyth for being the

first town in Britain to include students in the policy-making committee of the council, in 1971. In fact the only criticism of the Athenian aspect of the town expressed by visitors is directed towards the architecture of the old college: 'Some people profess to find Aberystwyth ugly and dull. It ... has a conventional sea-front [allowing] full attention to be paid to the frankly shocking architecture of the College, but it must be remembered that the College was the result of nationwide sacrifice.'

The writer should have also noted that the building had originally been planned as a hotel but the enterprise, which had cost £80,000, failed and the building was bought for the college for £10,000. This makes it a fitting emblem of Aberystwyth's twin function of tourist destination and seat of learning. The prolific travel writer, H.V. Morton somewhat condescendingly described this dual function: 'Aberystwyth, to a Birmingham man, suggests bathing, boating, and a day out at the Devil's Bridge, but to a Welshman it is the town where Blodwen is trying to be a teacher and where David is climbing out of the agricultural into the professional classes.' Morton also contributes to the ongoing attempt to describe Aberystwyth through comparison with another more famous place when he labels it the 'St Andrews of Wales'. One of the least complimentary comparisons is found in a 1949 book by S.P.B. Mais in which Aberystwyth is described as a 'Lilliputian Llandudno with a miniature Great Orme's Head.'

Travellers' accounts of Aberystwyth demonstrate the various roles the town has had and opinions held regarding these functions. Perhaps these many impressions of Aberystwyth emphasize change in the town at the expense of the continuity that also undoubtedly exists. Nevertheless, the many changes in the town's role depicted in observers' reports afford us a glimpse into the past of Aberystwyth and how the town has been perceived through the ages.

*Mr Benbough-Jackson*

## The Wealth of Aberystwyth

When you walk through Aberystwyth you realize that you are in the middle of a pleasant town; there are no small mean houses in Aberystwyth. In his lecture 'Government, Religion, and Politics' published in Aberystwyth 1277-1977, Ieuan Gwynedd Jones said that 'in the Welsh boroughs as a whole almost one half of the total electorate occupied houses of between £10 and £15 annual rateable value: that is to say the bulk of the electorate, judged by this criterion, were relatively the poorest or least prosperous part of the electorate. But in Aberystwyth only about one fifth came into this category. Hence, it was a fairly well-to-do electorate. Nor could one reasonably refer to any section of this electorate as 'working class'. In 1867 it was estimated that only 3 per cent of the Aberystwyth voters belonged to the working class. The members of the working classes whom one can identify through their connections with Friendly Societies and other such organizations (like the Reading Room or Literary Institute in Bridge Street, the centre of the 'working class district') are usually skilled men, artisans, shipwrights, labourers, craftsmen and apprentices rather than common workmen.'

When considering the history of Aberystwyth, it is essential to remember that it is, for the most part, too intricately entwined with that of the church and parish of Llanbadarn Fawr to be easily disentangled from it. Aberystwyth is essentially the town that is the 'face of Llanbadarn in the world', and there is a long tradition of great riches and lack of pomp in the history of this area. From early times the rich mines have been instrumental in creating powerful men, but tracing wealth is never easy. However, we know that John Gifford married Maud, the heiress to mines in the Vale of Perveth, which came under the parish of Llanbadarn Fawr. In the Welsh Assize Roll we see a legal battle between him and Rhys Vychan for title on Llandovery Hirfryn and Pervedd, which went on for years until, in April 1282, Gifford won. He was then one of the richest men in Europe.

If you go to Worcester, where he became bishop (his wife's tomb has been found beneath his in the cathedral), you will find

*Aberystwyth putting green, castle grounds, early 1900s.*

that he is still remembered as he changed the status of the diocese. Whereas before it had been a dual see as in the case of Bath and Wells, it went on to become a powerful bishopric in its own right. When I visited the cathedral some years ago there was a hotel being built in the city bearing his name because his great wealth had done much for the town.

At the end of the reign of Elizabeth I, Sir Hugh Middleton financed the construction of the 'New River' to take fresh water to London, from the profit, for one year, of the mines near Goginan. In his letter Lewis Morris, the King's surveyor, wrote that in the time of Queen Elizabeth I and James I Sir Hugh made £24,000 each year for several years from the silver produced by just one of these mines. After Sir Hugh Middleton's death Thomas Bushel amassed a vast amount of wealth, erected a mint at Aberystwyth, clothed the entire army of Charles I, made him a present of a regiment of horse and defended the island

of Lundy at his own expense.

Lewis Morris, writing in 1742, observed: 'They have raised at Darren Vawr Hill near Aberystwyth ore worth £16,000 a year. The expense to be deducted is about £4,000. So there is a clear profit of £12,000 a year all within the compass of 200 yards.' He goes on to say that he can form companies in London that, by exploiting the mines, can become 'as rich as Croesus'.

By the nineteenth century the world had found riches elsewhere, but the echoes still remain in Aberystwyth. The houses may not be models of perfection but there are no mean streets in the town. Even more obvious than the comfortable size of the houses, though, is the heritage of the intelligence and erudition of earlier ages. Lewis Morris obviously thought more of history, languages and religion than he did of wealth, though he treated that with respect. The men who followed him shared his love of learning. Aberystwyth is the home of the first University College in Wales and, built in the

*Llanbadarn Fawr church.*

twentieth century, the National Library must surely enjoy one of the most beautiful settings of any such building in the world.

*Pauline Vivash*

## The Cardi's Passion for Cows

Dairying has played an important part in the economy of most Cardiganshire farmers for at least two centuries. This can be seen by going through farmers' account books of the last few centuries. Mary Evans of Llanwenog recorded everything that took place on her farm from 1778, when her husband died, until she died in 1797. She wrote about a neighbouring farmer who kept two cows, selling two casks of butter in the course of a year. One cask sold for 5d per pound and the other for 6d per pound. The total money received for the two casks was £3 10 0, which was 10s 10d more than his rent. Another farmer's wife, from the same parish,

produced a cask of butter from her cow in one year. The selling price was £2, which was 10s more than her rent.

Cardiganshire farmers below the sheep walks were mainly cattle breeders and rearers. There were at one time about twenty yearly fairs in the county where local cattle were sold for fattening to the graziers on the rich English pastures. The majority of these fairs were within the watershed of the rivers Aeron and Teifi. Nine or ten of these fairs existed before 1700. The monks of Strata Florida started Ffair Rhos when they moved to their new Abbey in 1165. Another fair, in 1630, was at Talsarn in the Aeron Valley. Both these fairs continued to within living memory.

The usual farming pattern was for the cows to calve in early spring and the calves to be bucket-reared on fresh milk. The butter-making season started at about the end of April or beginning of May, when the calves were weaned onto skimmed milk. Dairying was entirely women's work, carried out either by the farmer's wife or a dairymaid; they tended the cows, did the milking and made the butter. At one time it was an insult to ask a man to milk a cow. The women had the assistance of the gwas bach or young lad, the lowest in the servants' pecking order, to do the heavier work such as mucking out.

The women took pride in the butter they produced and regarded butter-making as an art. Any young girl who went out to service on farms reckoned she had reached the pinnacle of her career when she became a head dairymaid. The butter trade lasted until the late 1920s. I have often wondered why the Cardi who went to London to make his fortune, with this background, usually found work in the milk trade. The Carmarthenshire lads always went into the drapery trade.

In North Cardiganshire the butter was sold mainly as 'pound butter', that is made up into pound or half-pound packs. Some was sold to the barracks, at the local lead mines or in Aberystwyth. The surplus was sold through dealers in South Wales. In South Cardiganshire some pound butter was sold but most of it was bought by butter dealers for blending, and forwarding to South Wales. Up to the end of the nineteenth century butter was stored and sold in wooden casks, or tubs, that were made by a local cooper or 'hooper'. The usual charge for a cask was between 2s 3d and 2s 6d. When complete, the weight of the empty cask was carved on the bottom. The usual weight was between 12 and 14lb when empty and 120 to 140lb when full; small tubs were 60 to 80lb.

The butter made during the summer was sold the following spring; only isolated sales were made in the autumn. One dealer has recorded seeing three years' butter all together in a farm dairy. The butter was

*Cow and dairymaid, Bontgoch.*

heavily salted so as to preserve it. The average price in the 1870s was about 1s 1d per pound and in the 1880s stood at around 10d per pound. The average amount of butter produced per cow was between 100 and 110lb a year.

At the end of the nineteenth century refrigerated ships were developed and began arriving from the Commonwealth with good quality butter, spoiling local trade for heavily salted butter. It was only the South Wales colliers and steel workers who kept up a demand for locally produced butter well into the twentieth century. The new taste in butter resulted in the butter dealers requiring only unsalted butter from the producers, which they then blended. This worked all right for farmers who could fill a cask in a week but when it took two or three weeks the top layer of butter would be sweet and the bottom would be very strong. For this reason the dealers started a weekly collection. The farmers took their butter to the nearest collecting centre or, as they were called, 'collecting stations', which could be a village, a farm, or even a crossroads out in the middle of the country. The new method of marketing put an end to the casks as it was more convenient for the farmer to carry the butter in a bucket that was kept especially for the purpose.

One of the largest dealers in mid-Cardiganshire was Peter Davies of Pont Llanio. In 1905 he bought a small building at Pont Llanio, which had been a small butter-making factory, and used it for blending and salting butter before sending it by rail to shops in South Wales.

According to his nephew, Percy Evans, 4 or 5 tons of butter was sent away every week during the summer. Several smaller dealers also sold the butter they collected to Peter Davies. In the Teifi valley the agricultural co-ops used to collect butter for the CWS in Cardiff. The cancellation of the CWS butter contract with the Llandysul Agricultural Co-operative Society led to the formation of Tivyside Creameries Limited and the opening of their creamery at Capel Dewi. Butter dealers also used to pay regular visits to local markets to meet the farmers.

Skimmed milk was mainly used for stock feeding, not only for the calves but also for pigs. I have heard of one farmer feeding it to foals when they were weaned in the autumn. This practice of stock feeding lasted well into the war years. When farmers used to send liquid milk to the creameries they brought back skimmed milk. During the late 1940s farmers realised that full-time milk production paid better than stock rearing and gave up buying back the skimmed milk.

Sometimes skimmed-milk cheese was made on a small scale but it was not very popular as the resultant cheese had a strong flavour and was very hard. A farmer in Llanbadarn Odwyn used to add goats' milk to the skim so as to improve the cheese. Though the cheese was not very popular, there had been two fairs where cheese was sold, namely Ponterwyd and Ystrad Meurig. The average price during the last half of the nineteenth century was about 3d per pound.

The main markets for Cardiganshire butter, as well as eggs and bacon, were the mining valleys of South Wales. Up to the second half of the nineteenth century they were delivered by horse and cart, which used to arrive at regular intervals in groups of ten or twelve. They not only came from this county, but also from Carmarthenshire and Pembrokeshire. Since the majority of these carts came from Cardiganshire they were called 'Cardi Carts'.

The Cambrian Railway from Shrewsbury to Aberystwyth was opened in 1864, and in

1867 was joined by the Manchester and Midland Railway, taken over later by the Great Western Railway from Carmarthen via Lampeter and Tregaron. Not only could the railway deliver more quickly and cheaply than Cardi Carts, but it could also deliver further afield, although the mining valleys still remained the biggest customer for many years.

During the nineteenth century demand for liquid milk in towns and villages was met by smallholders on the outskirts or by dairymen keeping a small herd in the towns. In London and other large cities herds of over a hundred cows could often be found in one large shed. They were kept tied up from the time they were bought until they became uneconomic to keep and then sold, usually to the local butchers. Milk was first brought into Manchester by rail in 1847 and shortly afterwards was transported by rail into London, but only in small quantities until the start of the cattle plague of 1865. During the spread of this disease hundreds of cattle died, especially in the large cattle sheds in the cities.

The market for liquid milk did not come to Cardiganshire until the early 1920s, and was sent mainly to London. A farmer from the Aeron valley used to take his milk to meet the train at Llanaerchaeron Halt by 6.20 a.m. every morning, to be delivered to the Mutual Dairies in London. Around 1930 the Mutual arranged for a lorry to collect milk from the Aeron valley for the new collecting centre at Carmarthen. The Milk Marketing Board took over the area covered by this dairy in 1936.

London was not the only market for Cardiganshire milk in the 1920s. The

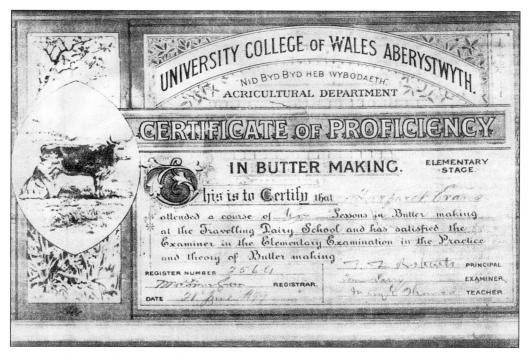

*Butter Making Certificate of Proficiency, University of Wales, Aberystwyth.*

*Aberystwyth, 1875.*

retired stationmaster at Pont Llanio remembers milk going to Swansea and Cardiff as well as London; it was always delivered in 17-gallon churns, although the farmer was paid for 16 gallons. The buyers insisted that there was half a pint of spillage in every gallon of milk delivered. Producers received about 8d per gallon, from which they had to pay the transport to the buyer's station. It was a buyer's market and there was often friction between the two parties which led to the formation of the MMB in 1933 to act as middle-man.

In 1932 the old Co-operative creamery at Newcastle Emlyn was re-opened by the Dried Milk Products company, taken over later by Cow & Gate, to manufacture cheese. Although it was on the Carmarthenshire side of the river Teifi, it collected milk from south-west

Cardiganshire as far north as New Quay.

A new co-operative creamery was opened at Capel Dewi in 1932 and the MMB opened a separating station at Pont Llanio in 1936. The opening of these creameries was a blessing for the farmers of the county during the hard times of the 1930s. During the late 1920s the country girls lost interest in finding employment on the local farms, resulting in a shortage of dairymaids. This, plus the new method of marketing milk, brought a new category of servant to the Cardiganshire farms, namely the cowmen or, as they are called today, herdsmen. They took over the dairy herd, including helping with the milking.

The old system of banking in Wales was by means of promissory notes and deposit receipts, a system hardly heard of in England. If a trustworthy farmer wanted to borrow from a bank he would have to sign a promissory note and pay the interest in advance. Usually the note would be for a period of three to six months. If the farmer could not repay in the given time he would have it renewed, again paying the interest in advance. If the money were deposited with the bank the farmer would receive a deposit receipt, signed by the bank manager and one other bank official. About every six months the receipt would be returned to the bank, the holder would collect his interest and the receipt would be replaced by a new one. This system of banking lasted with most Cardiganshire farmers until the coming of the monthly milk cheque.

Welsh Black cattle were kept throughout the county during the nineteenth century, but by the end of the century the farmers of south Cardiganshire had gone over to Shorthorns. The landowners in this area were practical farmers who took an interest in new developments in agriculture; they saw the advantage of the dual-purpose Shorthorns, which were earlier to mature than the native breed, and encouraged their tenants to buy bull calves from them for crossing their own cows. By buying an occasional pedigree cow, several farmers built up successful herds over a number of years. In the north of the country, the landlords were not interested in farming and their tenants did not get the encouragement to move with the times; the Welsh Black was therefore the dominant breed until well into the twentieth century.

The breeding policy started by the farming landlords was carried on during the period between the two world wars by 'bull societies'. Small groups of farmers co-operated to buy a bull under the Government Premium Bull Scheme. Bulls were usually North County Shorthorns, selected by the county livestock officer and bought with the assistance of a government grant. The popularity of the Shorthorn lasted well into the 1930s and then the Friesian gradually replaced it. By this time milk production was given priority and today the Friesians are the predominant breed on Cardiganshire dairy farms.

The numbers of farmers keeping a bull today are very low. The majority of them use the services of the Milk Marketing Board's artificial insemination centre at Felin Fach, or its sub-centres at Aberystwyth, Llandeilo or Newcastle Emlyn. The Milk Marketing Board began its AI organization in 1944 when it bought the North Suffolk Cattle Breeders' AI centre at Beccles. Felin Fach was first opened as a sub-centre to Carmarthen in 1949, becoming a centre in its own right in 1951. The centres have available a selection of over 150 bulls of forty different breeds.

The Milk Marketing Board organized several farm management services for the farmer, one of these being milk recording. John Spiers in Ayrshire started recording in 1903 but, although milk-recording societies were formed in most counties of England and Wales, it did not become popular for about forty years. In 1939 only 6 per cent of milk producers kept milk records. The Milk Marketing Board took over the responsibility of organizing milk recording in 1943.

The estimated average annual yield per cow a hundred years ago was 200 gallons, but the average today is nearer 1,000. When the Ministry of Agriculture started collecting agricultural returns in the 1860s there were 20,000 cattle in Cardiganshire. It was not until the 1950s that the records separated cows producing milk for sale or for rearing dairy

*Lluest Dairy milk deliveries, 1935.*

replacements, and calves destined for beef. There were 39,481 dairy cows in the county by 1967.

The economy of farming today favours a farmer with a large farming unit and there are numerous dairy herds of a hundred cows or more. The larger units are usually formed by uniting two or more farms and concentrating the housing and dairy on one site. In 1971 there were 1,953 dairy herds in the county, but by 1980 this had dropped to 957. Over the same period milk production had risen by 32 per cent to 3.85 million gallons (17.5 million litres).

The early 1950s seems to be the watershed between the farming practised between the two world wars and the highly efficient farming of today. This is the period when farmers started making a science of growing grass by studying the use of fertilizers and new strains of grass, and breeding for higher yields by careful selection of cows and stud bulls. This was also the time that farmers started to mechanize and the milking machine became a common sight.

Several attempts were made to provide agricultural education during the eighteenth and early nineteenth centuries. Oxford University had a School of Rural Economy as early as 1796, and a Royal Charter incorporated the Royal Agricultural College, Cirencester, in 1845. In 1887 a government committee decided that there was a need for instruction in modern methods of farming, resulting in Parliament allocating the sum of £5,000 to assist existing agricultural schools. Further help was given by the passing of the Local Taxation (Customs and Excise) Act in 1890. This Act made available to the county councils money for providing agricultural education and to employ a qualified agricultural officer who, with the assistance of advisors in poultry and dairying, provided technical instructions and advice for farmers.

Cardiganshire was very fortunate to have, as Chief Agricultural Officer, the late D.J. Morgan, a native of Llanddewi Brefi, who had qualified at UCW Aberystwyth. He held this position during both world wars and the period in between. It was due to his efforts that Cardiganshire became one of the first counties in Great Britain to be declared a clean area under the tuberculosis (attested herd) scheme.

At the beginning of the Second World War, the government set up a War Agricultural Executive Committee in each county. Their duty was to organize a programme for increasing food production. The Cardiganshire committee had D.J. Morgan as its secretary and appointed a group of qualified staff to help and advise farmers on technical problems such as draining, fertilizing etc. As a result of this advisory work the Government, in 1946, formed the National Agricultural Advisory Scheme. The service has its own experimental farms and laboratory services, such as Trawscoed in this county, to support the officers in the field. The NAAS created an interest for local farmers in new methods of farming that led to the opening, in 1952, of the Farmers' Education Centre at Felin Fach. This was to provide day release classes in agriculture for the county's young farmers and introduce computers as an aid to farm management. Since writing this the centre has been closed down.

In 1881 Professor Tom Parry was the first to organize courses in farm dairying at the centre in the University College of Wales at Aberystwyth. He also formed travelling dairy schools where dairy instructors went around the villages to instruct local girls in the art of butter making; they brought the equipment and the pupils brought their own cream. Those who showed a degree of proficiency in these classes were encouraged to take more advanced courses at the college. The University also supplied lecturers during the winter evening to instruct local farmers in general agriculture. In 1929 a farm institute was opened at Piberlwyd

*Cattle Market, Aberystwyth.*

near Carmarthen where many pupils from this county took the opportunity to improve their farming knowledge.

There have been many changes in dairying and education in the county since the beginning of the twentieth century. The 200-gallon cow has been developed into a 1,000 galloner; the market has passed from the mercy of the butter dealers to the guaranteed market of the Milk Marketing Board and the travelling dairy schools, with their butter churns, have become day-release classes and training in the use of computers.

*Ifor Jones*

## Alfred Worthington

Alfred Worthington is Aberystwyth's most prolific artist and is known to most people for his paintings of local scenes, especially Llanbadarn church. Many of his paintings are to be found in the Ceredigion Museum and the National Library of Wales.

In September 1885, Mr Worthington's eldest son, also called Alfred, had an accident while trying to negotiate the harbour entrance in his fishing boat *Providence*. In the collision, which damaged both boat and nets, Aberystwyth nearly lost her foremost artist who was aboard at the time with his son. To help his son out of his subsequent financial predicament, Mr Worthington raffled ten of his paintings, which were put on display in a shop in Eastgate. The raffle was a success and enough money was raised to make good the damage. The *Cambrian News* of the day commented rather ambiguously that 'some of the paintings are of real merit'.

While most people are aware of Alfred Worthington's connection with Aberystwyth, many details of his life remain a mystery. Much of what is known comes from the work of Mr Freeman in the Ceredigion Museum and from his obituary. Taking his obituary (probably written by W.R. Hall and based on an interview published in the *Cambrian News* in September 1923) as a starting point, this is an attempt to fill in a few gaps and build up a picture of his life.

Alfred Worthington was born in the parish of St Mary, Dover, on 14 September 1835 and was baptised on 21 October. His father was Lt Benjamin Worthington RN, who was later made a fellow of the Royal Society for his work in improving Dover harbour. Lt Worthington was a native of Dover and resided there all his life, except when engaged in naval operations during the Napoleonic wars. Both of Alfred's parents came from comfortable backgrounds; his mother, Mary, was in receipt of a private income, while his paternal grandfather kept the Ship Hotel in Dover and ran coaches from Dover to London. Young Alfred received art lessons, though these came to an end on the death of his teacher, whose identity is unknown. His mother's private income enabled him to live in the back woods of Canada for five years, indulging his hobbies of hunting and fishing. His obituary implies that this was some time in the 1870s or 1880s, though it seems more likely that it would have been before he married Elizabeth Ashtell Godden on 11 February 1862 at Trinity church, Dover. Alfred was about 6ft tall and of a quiet disposition.

During the 1860s the family was living in Guston parish, in a village which was subjected to an epidemic of cattle fever. A number of local children (including a child of the Worthingtons) died as a result of drinking infected milk. Alfred consulted Dr (later Sir) Morrell Mackenzie at the Greenwich Hospital as to the best course of action. (Sir Morrell Mackenzie (1837-1892) was one of the founders of the science of laryngology. At the time that he was working in London, one of Alfred's brothers, Edward, was a secretary to the Greenwich Hospital and so may have arranged the consultation.) Dr Mackenzie advised Alfred and his family to move to Aberystwyth for the bracing air of the Welsh coast, advice that with hindsight proved faultless, as Alfred Worthington lived to the good age of eighty-nine.

Alfred took his advice and bought No. 5 Queens Road, Aberystwyth. The first mention of his presence in the town was in the Aberystwyth Observer of 7 May 1870, when he made a donation to a fund established to send a local blind girl to a special school. In the 1871 census he is recorded as living in Queens Road with Elizabeth and their five children, and a servant born in Guston. He gives his occupation as artist, painter and photographer.

During his youth he had been a keen amateur photographer (another sign of the affluence of his family) and shortly after arriving in Aberystwyth he took over an abandoned photographic studio which had been established at No. 35 Marine Terrace by Hopwood and Co.

By September 1872 the ever-expanding Worthington family had moved to Terrace Road, in premises that had previously been a public house, the Bull and Mouth. It is now the site of Boots the Chemist. For a short while he retained the licence to increase the value of the property, but he did not run the premises as a public house; instead, it seems that he rebuilt the site and incorporated a photographic studio into the new building. In 1875 he is listed in a trade directory as a photographer and bookseller. Most of the carte de visite photographs taken by him carry his address as Terrace Road, and his obituary states that he lived in Terrace Road for twelve years. They were still at this address for the 1881 census, but had moved to Cambrian Place by August 1882. This was also the address given by his son, Edward, when he appeared in court charged with the heinous offence of playing cricket in the street in 1883 (he was fined 1s)! The move to Cambrian Place may have been prompted by his increasing involvement in decorating slate at one of the slate enamelling works. He is particularly noted for decorated fireplaces, frequently incorporating local views. Slate enamelling was a local speciality at the time, with five different firms involved. Alfred Worthington worked primarily for Messrs Morris and Jones, whose workshop was on the current site of Charlie's Stores. It is traditionally thought that he kept a photographer's studio on in Cambrian Chambers.

It was at about this time that the family's interest in commercial fishing developed. Alfred Snr entered into partnership with Captain Hughes, landlord of the Sailor's Arms, and purchased Eagle. Later he also owned

Marcus Moxham outright. His son Alfred, a lifeboatman, acquired his first fishing boat, the Providence already mentioned. During the 1880s the picture becomes more confused; one A. Worthington can be traced at addresses in High Street, Windmill Court and Moor Street, but it is not clear which Alfred Worthington these refer to. It is not impossible, therefore, that Alfred Snr did go to Canada at this time.

By 1891 he was living at 14 Vulcan Place, his occupation being given as Artist in Painting. He lived at this address until at least 1903 when his wife died. He is later said to have moved to a house in Clarach, which later became an isolation hospital. By 1920, he was living with his daughter, Ethel, at No. 17 Rheidol Place and continued to do so until his death on 1 February 1925, aged eighty-nine.

Alfred and Elizabeth Worthington had fifteen children in total, although only six outlived their father. Of the others, two, possibly three, died in infancy. Alfred Jnr died of a heart attack while trying to secure one of his boats in a storm, Charlie died in a yachting accident in Cardigan Bay and Edwin drowned in Hamburg. The fate of the others is not known.

*William Troughton*

## Hetwyr Tre'r Ddol – The Hat Makers of Tre'r Ddol

Welsh hats. Were the famous tall Welsh Hats authentic, or were they more in the style of a bowler? Why was their production a cottage industry confined within a limited parochial area?

During the first half of the nineteenth century the felt hat industry flourished in the parish of Llangynfelyn, and especially in the area around Tre'r Ddol although there is no

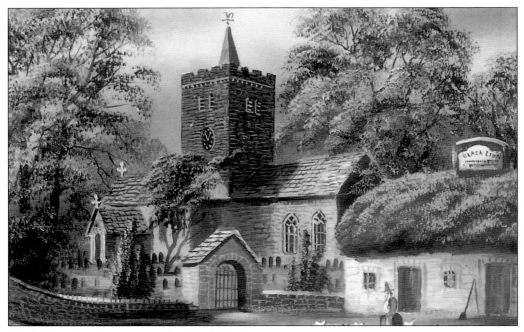

*Llanbadarn church, a painting by Alfred Worthington.*

trace remaining today. This industry made many dozens of people perhaps not rich, but at least substantially better off than their neighbours who were labourers or farm workers. The trade was based on a very few locations in and around the village of Tre'r Ddol where the existence of a 'melin ffelt' or fulling mill was recorded as early as the seventeenth century. The fleece of Ceredigion sheep was considered excellent for felt making. In some areas the sheep were shorn twice a year in June and October, the latter giving wool especially good for felt. Fur from rabbits and hares were also used – the former to make 'Sunday Best' hats and the latter for more workaday wear.

The process of making felt hats involved boiling the wool in huge vats of liquid containing vitriol and beer dregs, these supposedly reduced the toxic effects of the vitriol. The saying 'as mad as a hatter' refers to the fact that some hatters did indeed go mad because of the effects of the fumes. The felt was pulled over a block to shape it, then dried before being coated in shellac as waterproofing and dyed black. Finally it was smoothed with a hot, heavy iron. In 1826 a travelling Englishman passing through Tre'r Ddol noted 'several weavers' looms in the village and many black hat makers. Counted 31 hats drying outside one house.'

Various styles of hat were made including y cwcwll tal – the tall women's hat and special hats for miners and quarrymen which were designed to hold a candle. Prices were generally expensive. In 1834 a carpenter from Dole had a hat worth 8s in part payment for furniture he had made for long journeys over mountains and rivers, at a time when a corner cupboard would cost 18s. The hats were sold at markets across Wales and at quarries and coal pits. Until the railways arrived, in the mid-eighteenth century, they were carried in huge boxes strapped to the backs of the hat makers or onto donkeys for long journeys over mountains and rivers. Hats were heavy and there were approximately thirty in a load.

The name Edwards crops up often in connection with the industry. Isaac and Susannah Edwards were well known in Tre'r Ddol. David Edwards (Dafydd y Ffeltiwr) moved to Amlwch from Tre'r Ddol in 1820. His wife Elizabeth, y wreigen fach – the little woman, was known across Wales as it was she who travelled to market to sell her husband's hats. Most famous, however, was Thomas Edwards of Llety'r Fran. Born around 1754, he married Anne Evans in 1783 and, of their many children, all the boys were taught the hat making trade. Until his death aged eighty-seven, Thomas Edwards lived at Llety'r Fran, a farm on a back road above Tre'r Ddol. The old buildings, which housed his workshops, are still standing.

Among his sons were Thomas and Owen who married two sisters, Mary and Ann Jones, Ynyscapel. Thomas was a founder member of the Methodist establishment in the parish of Llangyfelyn. According to a land deed of 1831, Owen owned a 'hatter's workhouse and dye house' at nearby Gwyndy, and

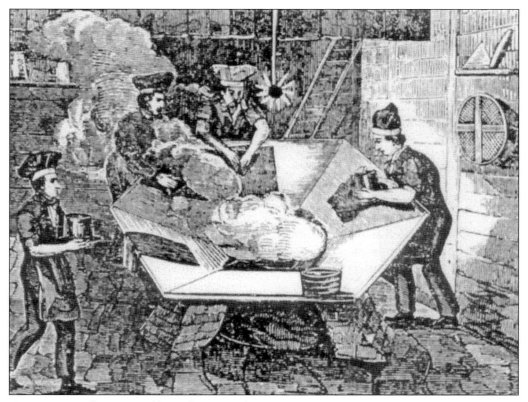

*Contemporary illustration of hatmakers at work.*

115

*Felt hats, before and after shaping.*

*Llety'r Fran, Thomas Edwards' home and workshop.*

made hats at the farm Ynys Tudor. Thomas junior had a workshop at Llwyn Wallter close by Llety'r Fran. It is likely that they farmed the land and hat making was part-time work. Slow poisoning from vitriol was not the only peril of the trade. A sword has been found at Llety'r Fran, which is thought to have been used by the family to protect themselves from robbers while journeying over the mountains to market. A tragic story is told of Lewis Edwards, son of the aforementioned Isaac and Susannah. He died on 14 August 1845 aged thirty, while carrying a load of hats from Tre'r Ddol to Caernarfon. When only three miles from his destination he dropped dead on the road, apparently overcome by the weight of his burden.

Owen Edwards had a son, a third Thomas, who moved to Llanfestiniog in 1830 where there would be a good market for hats in the quarries. He died in 1896 aged eighty. Other names recorded in the 1841 census as being hat makers were John Jones of Pantcoch, John Evans and James Jones at Goetrefach, David Jones in Llwyncrwn and others in Taliesin – over forty in all. By 1871, however, only five hat makers remained in Llangyfelyn parish, one, David Davies, being over eighty. A change in fashion was the cause of the sudden and abrupt decline in the industry. Silk hats were being manufactured in England which were lighter, smarter and cheaper to make and buy. They were carried on the new railways across Britain and sold in shops rather than markets. Milliners set up in business in the towns making ladies' fashionable hats from silk, wool and soft felt. The days of the hard felt hat were at an end.

In the absence of a visual record of this fascinating industry, we must endeavour to keep a written record of its existence within a very small and parochial area. Why it should have been so confined is not known and is a puzzle as interesting as the craft itself.

*Lesley Hughes and Anna Sistern*

## A Sad End to a Postmaster's Career

The first post office in Aberystwyth opened in November 1769 at premises adjoining St Michael's churchyard wall, the postmaster enjoying a salary of £4 per annum. In 1812 William Williams was appointed postmaster and he moved the post office to Market Street, conveniently next door to the Talbot Inn, from where the first mail coach left the town in 1807 for Ludlow. He was a prominent citizen, the father of Richard Williams, surgeon, who opened the first dispensary in the town.

On the death of her father on the 24 November 1824, Mary Williams became the postmistress. At Llanbadarn Fawr church on 25 June 1832, she married twenty-one-year-old Josiah Evans who described himself as an agriculturalist. On marrying, he was appointed postmaster at a salary of £40 per annum. The population of the town was 4,128. The new postmaster soon became friendly with James Hughes, a local solicitor who lived at Glanrheidol, and they regularly socialised at the St David's club where James Hughes was one of the committee members.

From the reports of the select committee on postage and parliamentary papers relating to the Post Office, the income of Josiah Evans, postmaster, is given as:

Salary
£40
Fees on late letters
£3
'Perks' on delivery of letters in town and beyond the fixed boundary
£7
Gratuities from private bags, Christmas boxes etc
£2 2s
Profits on money orders
£2

---

Gross income
£47 9s
Less office rent
£5
Other outlays*
£12

---

Net income
£30. 9s

* He had one clerk/stamper paid for by the Crown. The postmaster was also responsible for the salary of the letter carrier.

A letter from the postmaster of Lampeter, dated 11 June 1840, to James Hughes the solicitor, reveals for the first time that all is not well at the post office in Aberystwyth. The postmaster appeared to have mislaid a money order for five pounds, payable to Joseph Downie, and he was requested to inform the postmaster that there might be no further delay in the payment of the order. During this period one report stated that Josiah Evans had become addicted to spirituous liquor – having taken it at first on doctor's advice!

The General Post Office were now becoming concerned about the affairs of the postmaster as he seems to have got himself into financial difficulties, in fact they insisted that he put up two sureties to the sum of £500. He had no difficulty in getting his friend the solicitor to stand and Mr Hughes, who also represented the Earl of Lisburne, somehow persuaded him to stand as surety too.

On 11 November of the same year, a bailiff called at the post office and Josiah Evans' furniture and effects were distrained and deposited in the yard of the Talbot Inn next door, 'to be disposed of as the law directs', unless payment was received within five days. He owed £10 to his landlord, Mr James Rees, for two years' rent up to the 12 May. He must have received the bailiff with some displeasure, for he tried to destroy the inventory of the goods seized; it was, fortunately, recovered and pasted back together on the back of a blank post office form. The goods seized were:

**In the living room**
One square table
One sofa
One mahogany table
Window curtain
2 flower stands
One fender
5 pieces of carpet
Bottle stand and sundries

**In the bedroom**
Bed and bedding
One chaise
2 flower stands
Window cornice
Sundry boxes

**In the kitchen**

One square table
One chair and stool
One cast iron pot
One saucepan/one bellows
One tea kettle
Plates and dishes
5 bottles and sundries in cupboard
one clotheshorse
One tray and one fire stand
6 knives 4 forks 3 tspns

Josiah Evans was dismissed on 24 March 1841, and escorted to Cardigan jail as a debtor. The Post Office wrote the very next day to ask James Hughes to speak to the officer in charge of the post office at Aberystwyth, in order that arrangements may be made for the discharge of an estimated debt of £129 13s 10d due from him from the late postmaster.

Poor Josiah Evans, writing to his friend the solicitor from jail, was anxious to appear before the commissioners in order to obtain his discharge and did not expect opposition from any quarter. He trusted that the 'book debts' would be covered by arrangements made by his wife prior to her leaving Aberystwyth. He reckoned without the perseverance of the Postmaster General, who wrote to inform James Hughes that the amount owed had been increased to, 'about £200', and requested that immediate measures be taken for its repayment in order that the account with his department might be closed.

In July of the same year, the Accountant General of the Post Office, reported that the amount of £277 8s 3d due to his department from the late postmaster, still remained unpaid and begged to refer to previous letters on the subject. In November, in a letter to the Earl of Lisburne, the Post Office had the honour to inform him that, by the books of the department, the aforementioned sum, for which his Lordship was surety, still remained unpaid. Two weeks later, the Post Office regretted writing to his Lordship as it was found, upon further enquiries that his Lordship had withdrawn his responsibility as surety.

James Hughes must have taken heart from this news, for he wrote asking to be released from his responsibilities under the bond to the crown; and in reply the Post Office said it was out of the question. He asked for a reasonable time to make arrangements for repaying the debt and he was allowed a month, from 9 March 1842. Twelve months had now elapsed since Josiah Evans' dismissal and James Hughes had written again to the Postmaster General on the subject; he was informed that the first application was based upon 'estimate'. It distinctly stated that, although he could feel for the situation, he was not authorised to make any abatement whatsoever in the amount due under the bond.

The former postmaster still languished in Cardigan jail as it was the custom not to release a debtor until all that was owing had been repaid. In June the Post Office transmitted to James Hughes, at his request, a statement of the accounts of the former postmaster, noting that there was not the slightest reason to doubt their accuracy. On 30 November the Post Office, in a further letter to James Hughes, states that unless a communication on the subject of the debt was received by return of post, it would be placed in the hands of the solicitor to the department.

In February 1843, almost two years since the dismissal of the postmaster, James Hughes was still playing delaying tactics. The Post Office wrote to him to say that unless a very satisfactory letter was received 'by Monday next', the solicitor would be instructed to take proceedings for recovery of the amount due. Unfortunately, further correspondence on the subject has not come to light and it is assumed that the debt was eventually repaid, as James Hughes continued in practice in the town, as a distinguished solicitor, for many years.

Let us not forget Josiah Evans, who, one hopes, was eventually released from jail for, in a letter to his former friend, he assures him of his best exertions to repay him in full, as speedily as possible. The one person who could have given us the answer would have been Susannah James, who died on 3 January 1846, aged sixty years, and whose gravestone in St Michaels churchyard bears the inscription, 'for forty years in the Post Office department of this town', she was a letter-carrier and would have been employed during the whole of the unfortunate postmasters' tenure. Her salary was paid from his income.

*Ron Cowell*

# CHAPTER 5
## *Fiction from Fact*

*Aberystwyth, 1930s.*

## A Diary

Bridget Jones' Diary is now a hit movie based on Helen Fielding's novel, but what about Aberystwyth's own Bridget Jones? The story of our Bridget Jones – my grandmother – is somewhat different from the weight-obsessed, sexy career woman of the movie. She reared six boys in a tiny cottage in Poplar Row and in her early-married years sold fish from a hand-drawn cart around the streets. A penny each and 13 for a shilling! Although born some miles inland, at Melinbyrhedyn, in the Darowen district south of Machynlleth, Bridget had every reason to hate the sea. She forbade any of her sons going to sea and you will see why.

If this Bridget Jones had kept a diary, it could have read something like this:

1878
My father Owen Owens, dies aged sixty-one, before I am four years old. Mam is left with four of us children, my sister Margaret Elin only eleven months old, myself, my sister Mary, seven, and brother David, who is ten. Dad had been a lead miner and only married Mam fifteen months before I was born. He'd been married in Aberystwyth forty years ago and had two children by a woman called Winifred Griffiths, but they had long lived apart before she died in 1871.

**1879**

Mam and us children move down to Aberystwyth, coming by train from Machynlleth. Mamgu and Dadcu have come here from Darowen too, but they are old people. People used to call Dadcu, Jac y Crydd because he was a shoemaker at Darowen for years and years, though sometimes he worked in the lead mines around there. They live in Poplar Row near the little chapel we all go to, and Mary and I go to the National School in North Road where we must speak English, though we talk Welsh at home, of course. Mam can't read or write, but she does sums in her head and you can't cheat her.

**1880**

Mamgu dies on January 2 and is buried at Llanbadarn Fawr church, though we are Calvinistic Methodists. We are not sure of her age and they put sixty on the tombstone but it turns out she was about seventy-two. Poor old Dadcu lived less than a year and died a few days before my sixth birthday.

**1881**

We are now living in Skinner Street and Mam is a washing woman. My brother David is apprenticed to a painter, though he is only 13. Mary and I look after little Margaret Elin when we are not in school.

**1886**

What an excitement in town! Trefechan Bridge fell down after a great flood. It won't be rebuilt for two years, but people use rowing boats.

**1888**

Mam marries again. Our new Dad is a seaman in the merchant navy, John Jones, so we don't see him a lot. His two children, Robert and Ellen, both about seven, come to live with us in Skinner Street. The marriage doesn't last long because Dad is drowned off Tywyn a few

years later. Mam has to do lots of washing to make ends meet. She knows the seamen and takes to selling fish from a handcart.

**1897**

I am having a baby by a deep-sea seaman, Lewis Jones, from Castle Lane, Trefechan, and just after my twenty-third birth we get married. He is five years older than I am. Lewis's father works at Green's Foundry but his mother died years ago. Although Lewis is away at sea a lot, all over the world, he comes back for most summers, goes fishing and takes visitors out in the bay in a yacht.

**1904**

After having three boys, at last I have a beautiful baby girl and we name her Margaret, after Mam. Sadly little Margaret dies after only nine months.

**1908**

Mam dies on our eleventh wedding anniversary. The doctors say it was the asthma. She was sixty-for and we buried her in little Margaret's grave at the Aberystwyth Cemetery.

**1912**

My last boy is born. I've had six boys and one girl who died, and my sister Margaret Elin has six girls and one boy. My home is 7 Poplar Row, so seven must be my lucky number. Lewis has stopped going away to sea now that he is past forty and has got a steady job with the university college looking after the Old Assembly Rooms near the castle. We look after Ysgol Skin (the Sunday school).

**1918**

What a terrible war it's been. Only our eldest boy, David John, is back home after he was gassed at Ypres before he was twenty. He was blinded and lost his voice, but was later able to see with glasses. He eventually got his voice back when he went to a football match and shouted,

'Goal" without thinking he couldn't speak. Our second boy, Owen, was only fifteen when the war started but worked on the railways.

1926

The last of my boys, Brinley, leaves school as soon as he is 14 and Lewis gets him a job in the Department of Agricultural Economics at the university college. They are both in the old Green's Foundry building, Lewis looking after the boilers and Brinley a clerk with Professor Arthur Ashby. Brinley always hands over his wages to me every week and I give him something back, just like I did with all my boys.

1935

My brother David is killed when he falls from a ladder painting a house in Edgehill Rd. My son Willie identifies him for the inquest.

1939

Lewis, who survived going around the world four times on windjammers and in terrible storms through the Roaring Forties, manages to fall and break his leg in Great Darkgate Street. He doesn't get better and dies in hospital a few months after he is seventy. Four of the boys have left home and married now. None of them are in the Army or Navy in this war, I am glad to say.

1952

Here I am an old grandmother still living in the same part of Aberystwyth and the children call me Mamgu Poplar Row, though I am still Bridget Jane to my friends. Only one son, Idris, hasn't married and still lives at home. He works at the Plant Breeding Station. I still sweep out Ysgol Skin and help with the Sunday school and the parties. My two grandchildren in Northgate Street come to the Sunday school and play in the street during the week with their friends.

Endnote

Bridget Jones died in February 1953, aged seventy-eight, her life spanning six reigns. Her cottage was demolished in the 1970s for a car park but Ysgol Skin survives as a funeral home.

*Howard Jones (now living in Australia)*

## Elizabeth Davies

My name is Elizabeth Davies. The wind blows in the chimney corner, the fields lie white all around. There are three springs on top of the mountain: the Ffynnon Drewi – the stinking well, that is for things that don't thrive; the Ffynnon Rhewi, the freezing well, that is for healing infections; and the Ffynnon Di-rhewi, the well that doesn't freeze and will calm troubled spirits.

It is my wedding day; it drips with rain and the mist surrounds the cottage muffling sight and sound. I hardly dare to breathe behind the stacks of peat in the chimney corner, brownish bitter-smelling shreds of the stuff cling to my face and hair. This is my day.

I hear the men coming to the door, my mother and sister giggle with secrecy and excitement. The first verses are sung; Mam and Mari give the answering rhymes. Some scuffling and horseplay and the men enter the cottage. Of course they know that I am hidden here, but still a great play is made of searching the upstairs room, under the kitchen table, even in my sister's skirts. At last I am pulled out and I see my Dai at the back of the men. Off with us to the chapel and the minister for the proper part of the day.

If the minister knew what I carry under

my best Sunday skirts he would not smile on us so kindly.

The man walks out shutting the door as hard as he can. The sound of the wailing children follows him out into the fields. It's a beautiful bitter moonlit night, the clouds hurried across the sky by the freezing wind. The man walks carefully; his shadow hangs on the edge of the illuminated field. He chooses the animal with care, a weak one not so easily missed, and cuts its neck quickly. Blood stains the sodden ground as he moves back towards the cottage. It's not until the next day, when the feasting is almost over, that they come to take him.

When I was small, my Mamgu used to frighten me with stories of Whiti Bwli, brenin y mynydd, the king of Mynydd Bach. 'A great warrior who lives under the mountain', she would say. Countless years ago, he led the mountain men in battle against the men of the shore. Thousands were killed on that day and Whiti Bwli led his men victorious back to the mountain. There he lives to this day, waiting for the next great battle. But in the summer, when the weather is dry and he is thirsty and hot, Whiti Bwli comes out of his hollow and goes to drink from the Ffynnon Rhewi, walking the mountain in the shape of a great fox, the biggest anyone has ever seen, with teeth sharper than knives and eyes hot as the sun.

We live alone now, my lovely son Dafydd and me. My wedding day long forgotten, my man long gone to the coalfields without return. And so I join the many spinsters and 'widows', members of the desperate community who scrape a living up here on the cold mountain.

I hate the snow, the sound of the children shrieking and throwing, the way the wind howls in that way it only does when it snows. My Dafydd is only twelve years old and he's gone to be an apprentice with the carpenter in Llanfihangel. We've only had each other since before he was born. We don't bother with the chapel or the Cymdeithas now.

They come to my door in the early evening, the snow so deep the door won't open, and they have to kick it away. They are quiet while they do this; they don't speak. They stand in a group by the chimney corner and the councillor tells me his story, his nose is blue with cold and his eyes water. I want them to go from my fire but they keep telling me until I am supposed to understand.

As the carriage rattles away down the rutted track down to the richer lands below William sees the huddled cottages and huts grow smaller, clinging onto the damp hillsides. This is a place where you survive or submit to defeat; living would not be the right word. Imprisoned within this ungentle landscape, the people learn to exploit everything and anything within their reach: peat for the Aberystwyth bread ovens, moss for dressings and bindings, berries to be made into cordials which they will never drink.

Time is measured by cutting and stacking, Sunday school meetings and Cwrdd y Mynydd, births and deaths. The constant arrival of new people, eager to stake their claim to this place of venture, free of the rules of status and servility of the lands below.

William had come from that land, one of too many sons who had fallen in love with a girl from the other side of the mountain. They survived, in their own way. They didn't think about happiness or success, more about warmth, drying the clothes, and where the next meal might come from. He recites the names of all the houses under his breath like children, as they slip away from his sight.

It isn't true what they were saying. It's too far to travel from Llanfihangel each night so Dafydd stays there and I walk to see him once a month. It takes me four hours there and back, on a Sunday when everyone else is in chapel. I couldn't go this week; there was too much snow. No one could have done it.

On the day of his trial in Carmarthen Crown Court there was nobody there who knew him. 'You are a foolish man' said the judge, Lord George Rice, 'why did you not take a rabbit or a hare to feed your family, instead of stealing a sheep, which was the lawful property of the landowner?'

'I have a wife and ten children', William said,' the oldest a girl of 12, the youngest, twins of 9 months old. A rabbit would not feed my family. We were hungry'. There was silence.

They say my Dafydd has caught scarlet fever and died. They have buried him in the churchyard at Llanfihangel and this happened a week since, as the snow has been deep for so long that the news could not get to me. They could not carry the body of this boy home to lie in his local graveyard for the same reason. No one could have done it. This is some other boy, not my Dafydd. I feel such sorrow for that boy's mother, whoever she is. I will visit her when the snow has gone and I next walk over. I will keep watch now and not sleep until the snow has all gone.

On the day of his hanging William thought of his home, no more than a hut built by he and his wife with their own hands, the neighbours coming to help on the night, carrying mud and stone and uneven pieces of timber, and then sliding away at dawn as the smoke rose up from the holes still in the roof of knotted grass and earth.

Penbryn Mawr, Penbryn Bach, Troed y Foel, Pant yr Wyn, Lluest y Garn, Cefn y garn uchaf, Pant Y Clawdd, Pen y Bwlch, Tynewydd, Bryn-crwn, Minffordd, Llain, Pen y Banc, Ty'nddraennen, pentre, Ty'ncwarel, Ty uchaf, Ty'n rhyd, Lluest y Llwyni, sbeit, Pantyffynnon, Pant mawr, Pantamlwg, Llwyn'rhyddod, Panthwylog, Troed y Rhiw, Ty'n y Graig, Penwch, Pen Y Graig, Treweithan, Pen'rheol, Blaenhafren, Bron yr hydd, Brygwartheg, Ffwrdd Fach, Tan y Fron, Rhos Gron .

The snow has gone now, but I must still keep awake and say the words of the song my Mamgu taught me to keep Whiti Bwli away. They are bringing the body of a boy today to be buried in the graveyard. They say he has been taken from another grave and is being brought here to keep him from lying in a strange graveyard. I will go to the service, but I won't say Amen because that would mean it was true.

I will knit another pair of stockings to take to my Dafydd next time I go, grey as the skies, and blue as his eyes on a summer's day.

Afterword

Trefenter, meaning 'Venture town', is a hamlet on the inhospitable upper slopes of Mynydd Bach. During the nineteenth century it became the home of a host of squatters and smallholders, many of them building simple homes and claiming a small portion of land by the custom of Ty Unos, the one-night house. If they could build a house and have smoke coming from the chimney by the dawn, the house was theirs, their portion of land to be determined by the throwing of an axe.

There is a famous story of the War of the Little Englishman, an unfortunate man from Lincolnshire who bought the mountain from the Crown Commissioner in 1820 and attempted to fence off the common land. He was set upon by mobs of angry locals dressed in women's skirts and brandishing torches; having had two of his houses demolished by the mob, he eventually left. Such was the wild and desperate nature of this community, struggling for existence and to establish a community.

The interwoven stories I have told above, though less well-known, paint pictures of the reality of life of characters real and mythical that lived in Trefenter around the same time. Elizabeth Davies lived at Pant yr Wyn, Trefenter. Her only son Dafydd died in Llanfihangel Y Creuddyn and was re-buried in Trefenter in 1870. There is no record as to whether Elizabeth ever recovered from the mental anguish that afflicted her when her son died.

William Davies lived at Pistyllgwyn, Trefenter. He was hanged at Carmarthen in 1845 for the crime of stealing a sheep. The words that were said in court were recorded at the time.

Whiti Bwli, brenin y mynydd the king of Mynydd Bach is a mythical creature from the folk memory of who knows what past battles fought by tribal chieftains. The mineral springs were cleaned up recently and can be visited by those with a good map.

Unusual, though different, pre-wedding exploits still take place among the young people of the parish.

*Gill Ogden*

(*Sources: Ceredigion Library Oral History collection; Y Mynydd Bach a bro Eiddwen, Evan Jones; reports of the Cardiganshire Antiquarian Society; the stories of residents of Llangwyryfon and Trefenter.*)

## A week in the Diary of an English Lady c. 1822

Wednesday
Spent today quietly recovering from the tiresome journey from London. I ache all over after being bounced along terrible roads, squashed inside the coach with my brother; Anne, my companion; and two other gentlemen, who drank brandy from a flask and then snored loudly and mumbled for a good part of the way. Our apartment is clean and comfortable and the food is quite acceptable, I shall recommend the Talbot Inn to my friends.
Thursday
Today we ventured out to explore the town. My brother has bought us season tickets for the Assembly Rooms, which have not long opened, quite reasonably priced at 30/- for him, 20/- each for Anne and I. We passed them on the way to the castle ruins; I am looking forward to sampling the entertainments. The castle is a romantic place, most of it has fallen down but it still retains an impressive gatehouse with a portcullis and tower overlooking the sea. There is another tower, which is in a worse condition overlooking the town, and the remains of several walls and passageways. Beside the castle stands a small church called St Michael and all Angles. A pathway leads past the church to the sea, and next to that is a most wonderful house, designed by John Nash. It is called Castle House

and is right on the edge of the beach, its front door is at the back, with an elegant carriageway and triangular gardens on either side and turreted watchtowers. The main house has a castellated roof, and large windows which overlook the coastline to both south and north. I have been told that it was built for Sir Uvedale Pryce of Hereford. The fresh bracing air had tired us, so Anne and myself retired to our rooms early tonight. My brother went to the Assembly Rooms and came back late and quite merry.

## Friday

Today we walked by the harbour. It is quite small and is used mainly by small fishing boats as a sandbar prevents larger ships from entering. Across the harbour is a small village called Trefechan, which is separated from Aberystwyth by the river Rheidol. It has many lime kilns and I have been told that many rough people live there. This afternoon we went to the Promenade at the Assembly Rooms as it had started to rain. It is a fine building with a ballroom also used for the Promenade, with an area for reading, billiard room, a card room and a refreshment room. The Promenade was very pleasant with music provided be a small military band. There are some beautiful views here, I am glad I brought my watercolours with me.

## Saturday

A beautiful day today, I took my paints to Marine Terrace to paint Craig Lais this morning. I have noticed that there are a lot of poor women and children begging in the streets, I gave them some money, I felt so sorry for the children. My brother told me an intriguing tale about a man who used to work at this inn; he was told that this man, who was upright in manner with an unlined face, had claimed to be 117 years old. He had been known as 'the doctor' and regularly shaved visitors there.

## Sunday

We decided to attend the church by the castle this morning and my brother accompanied us. I wore my muslin dress and my high leghorn bonnet with the green veil and coloured ribbons. I sat next to a local woman who was very warmly dressed. She wore a grey stuff dress with a large shawl and a long thick blue cloth coat. On her head she wore a mop cap, a black silk handkerchief tied under her chin and a low black beaver hat. My brother was also fashionably dressed but he was completely outshone by a fellow who paraded himself like a peacock and stood up all through the service with everyone looking at him. He was wearing a short coat with such narrow skirts that they could not serve the purpose for which skirts were intended. He was obliged to carry his prayer book in his hand as the ladies do. His coat collar was low and topped with a huge cravat which was again overtopped by a stiff collar which was cut in the shape of a scimitar, and so high that it touched his ears and from the side obscured the bottom half of his face. His coat sleeves were short, but his shirt cuffs, which had an embroidered border, and extended well over his hands, were as stiff as his collar. His pantaloons, which were very bulky, were white. The church has a gallery, and musical accompaniment is provided by a barrel organ. A young man sat beside it and turned the handle while we sang hymns.

This afternoon we went to the castle grounds and I did some sketches. After supper we walked along the beach before retiring.

## Monday

Today we explored the Bath House next to the beach. It is a wonderful place, far nicer than I expected. The heated seawater is supplied to several tiled bath and shower rooms upstairs. There is a lovely sitting room with large windows overlooking the castle. It also has a dining room and some bedrooms. The rooms are beautifully furnished with fine paintings and engravings in every one.

## Tuesday

This evening my brother took us to a ball at the Assembly Rooms. The rooms are run to a strict set of rules and a gentleman wearing boots was refused admission, only military gentlemen are allowed to wear boots. Anne and myself were obliged to draw a ticket as we entered and our names and numbers were recorded in a book. Once you have drawn a ticket it cannot be changed and this sets the order for the dancing. In the card room it costs 12/- to buy two packs of cards, or 6/- for one pack, you are not allowed to use your own pack. No person is allowed to use cards left by another person and games of Hazzard are not allowed. Card playing is allowed to continue on ball nights after midnight but only as long as the dancing continues. We had a very pleasant evening and met some good people. I think I am going to enjoy the season here and will recommend a summer season in Aberystwyth to all my friends.

*Eileen Mullet*